BACK TO THE FAMILY

BACK TO THE FAMILY

Food Tastes Better Shared with Ones You Love

Art Smith

with Michael Austin

Published by

THOMAS NELSON

Since 1798

To my beloved Oprah Winfrey and Stedman Graham,
with love and appreciation, this book is for you.

———◄○►———

Recipes copyright © 2007 by Art Smith
Photographs copyright © 2007 by Stephen Hamilton

Published in Nashville, Tennessee, by Thomas Nelson, Inc.

Thomas Nelson, Inc. titles may be purchased in bulk for educational, business, fundraising, or sales
promotional use. For information, please e-mail SpecialMarkets@ThomasNelson.com.

Photographs on pages 58, 60, 66, and 121 by Tate Hunt for Stephen Hamilton, Inc.

Library of Congress Cataloging-in-Publication Data

Smith, Art, 1960-
Back to the family / by Art Smith with Michael Austin ; photography by Stephen Hamilton.
p. cm.
Includes index.
ISBN-13: 978-1-4016-0289-5
ISBN-10: 1-4016-0289-4
1. Cookery, American. 2. Family. 3. Menus. I. Austin, Michael, 1966 Dec. 28- II. Title.
TX715.S651317 2007
641.5973—dc22
2006039005

Printed in the United States of America
07 08 09 10 RRD 5 4 3 2 1

contents

A Tribute to Anne E. Bloomstrand

On life's journey we meet many people, and many of them we never see again. Some, however, leap directly into our hearts and never leave. It's hard to explain, but you know it when you feel it. We do not always know what brings us together, but with certain friends, as our relationship matures, we realize we are experiencing a unique feeling of love for a very special person.

It is only natural that when we find that "sweet spot" in a friendship, we tend to search for other people who will give us that same amazing feeling. Eventually we realize that God gives us only a few of those special people in a lifetime. I think of these people as earthbound angels who enrich our lives with their love. Unfortunately, we never know how long they will be with us.

My beloved Annie B, my first real friend in Chicago, came to me many years ago, and what an amazing woman she was. Her ability to bring people together through food was incredibly inspiring. She cooked as if she were a chef trained at the most prestigious cooking schools, but her food also had the unmistakable taste of the finest home cooking. I will always remember her dinners and listening to her tales of discovering the perfect vegetables for a particular dish at Chicago's Green City Market or a roadside stand out in the country. I will also cherish her stories about her children, Kristen and Scott.

To share a mutual passion with someone you love is one of life's great rewards. I will always be thankful for everything Annie gave us—from her words of wisdom that soothed our souls, to her unforgettable food that brought us so much pleasure. We will miss her, but in her honor we will continue the tradition of preparing beautiful meals for the people we love.

I love you Annie B, and I know that God now has the best cook in heaven. I can only imagine what great meals you are serving! Thank you for being our beloved colleague, family member, and friend. Thank you for sharing your life and your beautiful food.

CHAPTER 1

Finding Your Family in the World

I f we are lucky, in our ever-changing world, family is one thing that holds constant. Coming from small-town America and having planted myself squarely in the urban bustle of Chicago, I am constantly amazed at how readily the human spirit adapts to change.

Kindred Spirits

Growing up I had no idea so many people could live so closely together! But in the glorious crowds and life-affirming energy of my new hometown, I have found that similar interests and love have attracted people like me. We always seem to find each other. In the South we have a word for it—*kin.* And yes, technically it means those who share a common ancestry, but in a broader sense it also refers to people who think like we do, feel like we do, and love like we do. Kindred spirits. If we are lucky, those people become the fabric of our new families.

If we are lucky, in our ever-changing world, family is one thing that holds constant.

—Art

That is what happened to me, as soon as I realized it was possible for me to love others the same way I love my family in northern Florida. These newfound friends became my new family. What I found interesting was how many of these new friends came from similar situations and how many of them traveled around the world to live in America and raise their families in Chicago. We share a passion for our art and recognize the sacrifices we have made to achieve our dreams. We also have a common love for our families "back home."

Chicago

Chicago is a place packed tight with concrete high-rises and hard edges, but it is also smack dab in the center of the Midwest, where miles and miles of some of the world's most fertile growing soil separate the major metropolitan areas. Because of this, Chicago's edges are softened by a Midwestern sensibility fostered by the farmers who have fed the nation for decades.

Chicagoans are hard-working people who understand and appreciate good meals shared with friends. If they weren't, I wouldn't be able to get along with them! They have celebrated my cooking, and their Midwestern sensibility has kept me in Chicago, a place where you can rise to the heights of your full potential but still not be ashamed to serve a humble homemade biscuit.

Outside of Chicago, in the patchwork fields of the big-hearted Midwest, you find people not too unlike the people I knew growing up. Some of these folks—from Wisconsin, Michigan, Iowa, and other rural parts of the country—have found their way to the big city. I've always believed that people who have lived close to the earth have an appreciation for life and a humbleness about them. I enjoy being around people who know what a fresh tomato picked off the vine tastes like, or what it's like to help a heifer give birth to a calf—even if they haven't done it in thirty years!

I've always believed that people who have lived close to the earth have an appreciation for life and a humbleness about them.

—ART

When you are in a business so directly affected by the weather, as chefs and farmers are, you really understand and accept change. And you adapt. Sometimes you find yourself far away from where you started out, but somehow you know you are in exactly the right place. Like my mother, Addie Mae, says, "Honey, it's meant to be!"

The Family Farm

My life began on a farm, the same farm on which my great-grandmother raised many children, the same farm that to this day provides for our family. When I first wrote *Back to the Table: The Reunion of Food and Family*, which started this journey, I was not sure if people really would want to hear my stories about life in rural northern Florida. But my beloved family and friends told me to follow my heart. So I did just that. As a result, people have celebrated my stories and cooked from my book, and it is in that same spirit, with their support and love—and of course, with mine—that I bring you *Back to the Family*.

Celebrating Our Loved Ones

As we grow older, settle down, and form relationships, the razzle-dazzle of our passion feels empty without having our loved ones with us to appreciate it. Success is

wonderful, but sharing a meal with people you love is timeless and one of life's most fulfilling pleasures. Are you taking the time to play with your dear children or pets? Don't even get me started! When my kitties and puppies nudge my feet with their little noses, it inspires me to reassess my priorities and just slow down and accept the love from all the other lives important to me.

Life moves fast—too fast now and then—so don't forget to take the time to cook a meal for yourself and invite those you love to the table. Enjoy every morsel of it! You will find, as I have, that food always tastes better when it is shared with people you love. And it's even better when you call those people "family."

Time is the crucial element these days. Technology has allowed us to do more in a shorter amount of time, and because of that we are stretched even thinner than we ever were. Along the way, digital Blackberries became more important to us than ripe, juicy blackberries. In business, time is money. But in our personal lives, time is love.

We sacrifice our time for the sake of our loved ones, and that is one thing technology has not changed. Mothers and fathers plan their lives around the busy schedules of their children, thinking that the more their children see and do when they are young, the better they will be as adults. It is all done with good intentions, but we also need balance in our lives. We need to slow down and mark certain occasions with a nice meal and some kind words. We need to remember birthdays and anniversaries of all kinds. We need to find reasons to celebrate our victories with a homemade cake or a bottle of champagne. We need to remember what is important.

As we grow older, settle down, and form relationships, the razzle-dazzle of our passion feels empty without having our loved ones with us to appreciate it.

—Art

My ancestors used the *Farmers' Almanac* to determine when to plant and when not to plant. That was their technology. We have moved far away from that old lifestyle, but we also have realized that many of the things our ancestors held dear have value today. We have realized and accepted the importance of eating natural, healthy foods. And we have learned that sometimes doing things the old-fashioned way is better than the way we do things now.

How do we determine what is really important? As we grow older we realize that getting ahead has its pitfalls. Personally, I miss having a month with nothing to do. I miss simply going about at my own pace and not having to worry about events and meetings and deadlines. There is something to be said for just nothingness now and again—to be quiet, alone, and reflective. It is refreshing to be around people who do not need a single thing from us. Sometimes love does not require a word, but only a look.

With love there is forgiveness, but why put your love to the test? Slow down, refocus, and rededicate yourself to your loved ones. Remember their birthdays. Celebrate their victories. Or simply invent a reason to get together and mark an anniversary. Call it your five-year anniversary as friends, or anything else that is appropriate. Everyone wants to be remembered and celebrated. And now that you have that Blackberry, you have no excuse for letting one of these opportunities pass by you.

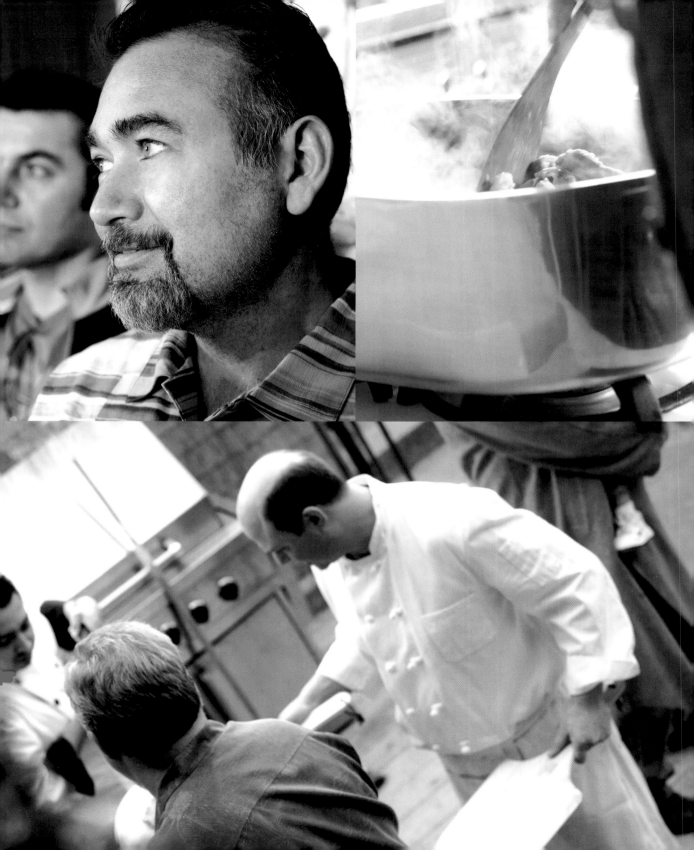

CHAPTER 2

Bless the Home and the Kitchen

The most sacred of all places is home. Wherever you go, your home remains the precious space that provides shelter, safety, and comfort at the end of the road. Lord knows, I have seen my share of homes. I have traveled the world cooking in people's houses, and I am constantly amazed at how people create their own personal comfort zones.

A home is more than just a place to hold your furniture and knickknacks. The concept of home is something we feel inside of us, not something we can necessarily see with our eyes. We all have a need on some level to create our own personal sanctuaries. A family heirloom can remind us of loved ones who have gone before us. In a similar way, a newly found object can remind us how far we have come, and possibly where it is we want to go. Those "things" can provide us with great feelings and inspire our creativity, but the heart of every home I have lived in has been the kitchen.

The Heart of the Home—the Kitchen

The kitchen is where we all come together. Feeding each other is one of the most sacred acts we as humans share. We cook for each other to nourish our bodies, and to demonstrate our love. I am thrilled to discover the different ways families decorate and personalize their kitchens. I am also saddened when I see empty refrigerators and cooking tools that have not been used. Those hanging clusters of pots and pans look good to me only if the pots and pans show a little wear and tear.

The Joy of a New Kitchen

This year I built a beautiful kitchen that would enable me to cook not only for my family but for my extended family, too. It has changed my life. This sacred place was not built overnight. I had been working for years in some of the most finely appointed home kitchens in the world, and then coming home to my simple apartment galley kitchen in Chicago. In my midforties I decided to settle down and buy myself an expansive home with room for the kitchen of my dreams. I wanted a place that would bring me comfort and at the same time allow me to bring comfort and joy to others. I found it.

The Italians are credited with creating cuisine as we know it today. They also happen to create some of the most beautiful kitchens in the world. So I turned to them to make my dream come true. Daniel Lagarth, Kevin Fitzsimons, and Gregory Herman of the Varenna Kitchen division of Poliform U.S.A. expedited the building of my kitchen. A sleek and amazing space replaced my dark kitchen. I could cook wonderful food in the old space, but I wanted a room where people could gather to enjoy meals together. Sharing what I love gives me more pleasure than keeping it to myself.

Feeding each other is one of the most sacred acts we as humans share.

—Art

Varenna succeeded in creating the most sublime, understated, sophisticated, creative cooking facility I could imagine. We hold charity dinners in my kitchen, including events for my children's program, Common Threads. Our mission at Common Threads is to provide a sanctuary for children so that they might discover ways to embrace their diversity and differences. Using food and the arts as our vehicles for change, our children teach, learn, share, and embrace all of our "common threads." I love bringing people into my kitchen and telling them all about these wonderful children and their tremendous victories. As church ladies in the South have known for years, offering food is the best way to get your point across. And having a great kitchen in which to prepare and serve it makes all the difference.

A great kitchen in a warm, open home is central to family. I also support Habitat for Humanity, which helps create homes for people in need. We all deserve that sacred place to call our own. Children need a loving home to feel comfortable and safe, and to develop into strong adults with a firm footing on life. We adults need a place like that, too. Wherever you call home, the most important thing is to fill it with love. Give thanks for what it provides for your family, and speak blessings over it and also ask others to bless it. Just make sure to treat it as the sacred place that it is. Here is a selection of my favorite blessings.

Always remember to forget
The things that made you sad.
But never forget to remember
The things that made you glad.

Always remember to forget
The friends that proved untrue.
But never forget to remember
Those that have stuck by you.

Always remember to forget
The troubles that passed away.
But never forget to remember
The blessings that come each day.

—TRADITIONAL IRISH BLESSING

May the road rise to meet you.

May the wind be always at your back.

May the sun shine warm upon your face.

And rains fall soft upon your fields.

And until we meet again,

May God hold you in the hollow of His hand.

—TRADITIONAL IRISH BLESSING

It is very nice to think
The world is full of food and drink,
With little children saying grace
In every Christian kind of place.

—R.L. STEVENSON

May the roof above us never fall in.
And may the friends gathered below
it never fall out.

—TRADITIONAL IRISH BLESSING

CHAPTER 3

Church Suppers and Pancake Breakfasts

I simply cannot think of the First Baptist Church of Jasper without thinking of my mother's potatoes. Whether it was her famous potato salad or her fresh green beans with new potatoes, Addie Mae always seemed to come up with new, delicious dishes. And believe me, every dish at those church functions was swiftly judged. Dealing with all those church ladies, it is a wonder my mother never lost her religion!

I love the song by R.E.M., "Losing My Religion." Now, there's a song you can cook to—perfect for a stir-fry or a vegetable chopping session for a giant pot of spicy chili. Cooking is a beautiful thing and one of God's greatest gifts to us. Food is also a gift, and having respect for it and giving it the attention it deserves is so very important. I was always amazed at how the women of our church made all that glorious food and still had time to attend service.

Church suppers bring people together. I can remember them drawing out people I hadn't seen in a heap of Sundays. I must admit, though, that many times sitting in those pews, I wasn't exactly there either. Preacher Martin was an old-time Baptist minister, and often his sermons lasted a full hour. I used to time it perfectly so that I was awake during the early singing parts and again at the end for the closing hymn. What a peaceful little sleep I was able to have each week, only to be nudged by my grandparents, Georgia and Palmer, for snoring.

My brother, Gene, would sit up in the balcony so that the preacher could not see him sleeping. Our poor mother would be so embarrassed. There she was—up in the choir loft—with one son snoozing in her midst and another son sawing logs in a pew below. Oh, how I loved to sing, though. And watching my mother sing up in that loft inspired me to do my best. My mother used to say, "Darling, the whole church could hear you." Thank God I had good pitch! Not to be disrespectful, but some of those preachers were so off-key it's a wonder God didn't send them packing.

After church, my friends and I would run to the church hall and marvel at the endless tables topped with every kind of covered dish known to churchdom. Churches were judged by the quality of their supper—or as we called it, "dinner on the grounds—although I can remember only one time when we actually had an outdoor picnic. It was just too hot for that kind of affair. Besides, the flies in North Florida look like small birds.

These feasts featured multiples of everything, with a lot of whispering about whose aunt had made which dish. In the South there is a charming tradition of beating around the bush so that when a dish is bad, really bad, you never hear about it. That is, you never hear about it until you go down to the 112 North Hately beauty salon, where Keith verifies word-for-word what was said by Mrs. So-and-So about dish such-and-such. I so love the South and its fine art of gossiping. It's never meant to hurt—only to entertain.

One of my favorite church meals was pancakes, served for breakfast or supper. The men of the church always cooked these meals to raise money for the local chapter of the Lions Club. There is nothing better than homemade buttermilk pancakes made with White Lily flour. These soft, light, and spongy cakes were delicious on their own, but when they were smothered in homemade cane syrup they were heavenly! Aunt Jemima did not live in my house, and she did not attend my church, either. I was weaned on homemade cane syrup and to this day, it's all I can eat on my hotcakes. The same goes for savory homemade sausages. When those wonderful links are swimming in syrup you get spicy, salty, and sweet all in one bite. Divine!

On Wednesday nights in Jasper we had the opportunity to get a midweek dose of God, so that by the time we made it to the weekend we were still feeling full. It was the religious equivalent of lunch, I suppose—or "dinner" as we called it. The best Wednesday was the first one of the month when there was a wonderful church supper. My grandmother Georgia would make her delectable chicken and rice, or "perlo" as

we called it. Perlo was rice made sticky by the protein from chicken bones, and hers had tiny bits of tender chicken spread all through it. On days when the preacher's sermon did not help me see God, Georgia's chicken and rice certainly did. (See Bettye's recipe on page 187. It's almost identical to Georgia's healing recipe.)

Her chicken and dumplings could do the same thing. My goodness, those tender dumplings soaked in that wonderful fresh chicken broth were so amazing that I still cook Georgia's recipe today when I want to feel close to her. What a great woman she was. She was with me all through my childhood, and even though this may be hard to believe, she was like a sister to me. We rode together to piano lessons in nearby Madison, and told stories and laughed. We worked in the garden together, picked fresh sweet corn, and then shucked it. Then she would cook it for me in a skillet and call it "fried corn."

Food has been and always will be an important part of bringing people together in search of God and enlightenment. Do you have something important you want people to hear? Offer to feed them and they will be there. (I also have a personal belief that preachers simply love to eat, and that's why they host all those church suppers!) In recent years I have attended other churches and observed the invasion of KFC and other prepared foods. All I can say is, *why?*

Homemade fried chicken, Baptist churches, and the South—those three things were meant for each other. All you church ladies and gents out there, keep making those wonderful foods and remember that even though you do not do the preaching, your food surely does. I so appreciate all the wonderful food that was prepared and served to me all those years in Jasper.

Regardless of your beliefs, just remember that if you want to bring people together for a cause, host a dinner or a supper and you will have no problem filling seats. People will come and celebrate. Once you have "captured" your audience, don't forget to tell them why you've gathered them together.

CHAPTER 4

Relishes—Finger Food of the South

In the South, calling little bits of food served before dinner anything except "relishes" is considered "highfaluten." Or as my southern brethren would say, "Puttin' on airs."

In my boyhood home of Jasper, Florida, a woman's status was directly proportionate to the deliciousness of her deviled eggs. Okay, that's stretching the truth a little bit, but make no mistake—deviled eggs are serious business in the South! When there was a church supper in Jasper, deviled egg plates would be lined up all along the buffet, and what fun it was to watch folks trying to sneak a look at the bottom of those plates. No one—I mean no one—in the South takes a dish to a function without putting their name on the bottom of it. And you do *not* want to get caught taking someone's plate by mistake and not returning it within the appropriate time.

Some of my fondest memories were made at the First Baptist Church of Jasper, Florida. At weddings there, it did not matter how large or how wealthy the host family was, the same fare was always served. There was always a variety of tea sandwiches, including cucumber, pimento cheese, tuna salad, and my all-time favorite, egg salad, which always makes me think of home. The only way to discern that a family had means was the size of the cake. The taller the cake, the closer to God, I guess. My goodness, there were some tall ones—a few so big that they even toppled to the floor!

The ladies of the church always made the food. No one thought of hiring a caterer in those days. Cooking was, and is, a way for people to show their love. It is a heartfelt

gift to a glowing bride or a gesture of respect to those in mourning. There is not a more gracious gift than food prepared lovingly by your own two hands.

As those darling church ladies prepared their specialties through the years, it was extremely satisfying to notice the pride they took in new discoveries. I remember in particular when hot pepper jelly on cream cheese arrived. Wow, now that was a culinary discovery! Serving sweet homemade chile pepper jelly with cream cheese had been beyond anyone's thinking. Then one day someone smeared the two on a Ritz cracker and created a taste sensation! I thought serving something so spicy at church might be just a little bit sinful. If it was—believe me—those people were committing a lot of sin!

Some of my fondest memories were made at the First Baptist Church of Jasper, Florida.

—Art

But probably a bigger sin, in the South anyway, is referring to a relish as an hors d'oeuvre, starter, canapé, or worst of all, *amuse-bouche*. The ultimate sin to a southerner is to forget the absolute goodness of simple food prepared lovingly and served in a dish with your name on the bottom.

MOST SOUTHERNERS SERVE THIS FINGER FOOD on proper relish trays placed on the dinner table before the rest of the food. Typically a southern relish tray includes black olives, green olives stuffed with pimientos, sweet pickled cucumbers or green tomatoes, and celery stalks smeared with creamy cheddar cheese. And to do it right, deviled eggs are served on a specially designed plate!

Church Lady Deviled Eggs

Growing up at the First Baptist Church of Jasper, Florida, I loved these wonderful eggs prepared by the ladies of the church. They are just as good today.

1	dozen hard-boiled eggs	4	tablespoons mayonnaise
2	tablespoons pickle relish		Salt to taste
1	teaspoon prepared yellow mustard		Paprika

1. Slice the eggs in half. Carefully scoop out the egg yolks into a bowl. Mash the egg yolks with a fork.

2. Add the pickle relish, yellow mustard, mayonnaise, and salt. Beat the egg mixture with the fork until creamy.

3. Spoon the egg yolk mixture back into the cooked whites.

4. Sprinkle with paprika and refrigerate, or serve immediately.

Pimento Cheese Spread

MAKES 24 TEA SANDWICHES OR 3 CUPS SPREAD

In my beloved South, there is not a reception without pimento cheese spread, either served in tea sandwiches or piped onto celery spears. This savory spread is loved by people of all ages.

1	bell pepper, roasted, peeled, and seeded	1	teaspoon Tabasco sauce
2	cups grated sharp cheddar cheese	1	teaspoon Worcestershire sauce
1	cup homemade mayonnaise		Pinch of salt

1. Finely chop the roasted pepper, then squeeze the pepper pieces lightly in a paper towel.

2. Place the chopped pepper in a bowl and add the cheese, mayonnaise, Tabasco, and Worcestershire sauce. Season with a pinch of salt.

3. Refrigerate for at least 2 hours before serving. (Chilling overnight is even better.) Serve on multigrain bread and add sprouts, or serve with celery stalks as they do in the South.

Pickled Green Tomatoes

MAKES 4 QUARTS

In the South pickles became very popular during the eighteenth century. These green tomato pickles always find their way onto relish trays. If you pick more than you need, fry the rest and enjoy.

1	gallon green tomatoes (16 cups sliced)	4	cups sugar
¼	cup canning or pickling salt	2	tablespoons pickling spices
2	tablespoons powdered alum	1	teaspoon allspice
2	cups boiling water	5	(1-inch) pieces fresh ginger
3	cups apple cider vinegar	4	cinnamon sticks
1	cup water		

1. Thickly slice the tomatoes. Place them in a large bowl, sprinkle with salt, and allow to sit overnight. This draws out the moisture to make your pickled tomatoes crisper.

2. The following day combine the alum and boiling water. Pour over the tomato slices and allow to sit for 25 minutes. Drain the tomatoes and soak them in cold water for 5 minutes. Drain them again and pack into sterilized hot canning jars.

3. In a clean stainless steel pot, combine the vinegar, water, sugar, pickling spices, allspice, and 1 piece of ginger. Bring to a boil, then carefully pour over the green tomatoes in the mason jars. A canning funnel makes this step easy.

4. Leave ½ inch of headspace and remove the air bubbles by gently tapping the side of the jar. Add 1 cinnamon stick and 1 piece of ginger to each jar. Wipe the jar rims and adjust the lids, then place in a large pot and cover with boiling water. Water level must be 1 inch above the jars. Bring the water to a boil, then cover. Allow the jars to process in the boiling water bath for 10 minutes. Very carefully remove the jars with a jar lifter or sturdy tongs. They're hot!

5. Place the jars on a wire rack or dish towel. *Do not retighten screw bands.* Allow the jars to cool 12 to 24 hours before putting them away. Jar lids will pop as they cool. If the center of the lid is indented, the jar is sealed. If the jars do not seal, store them in the refrigerator. Pickled green tomatoes will last several months in the refrigerator if sealed properly and only one month if not.

Marinated Olives

MAKES 8 SERVINGS

In Chicago I host supper almost every Sunday, and these olives are one of my favorite relishes to serve. They're simple, wonderful, and everyone loves them.

2	cups good-quality pitted black olives	2	tablespoons chili flakes or hot chili sauce
2	cups mushrooms, blanched		Zest of 1 lemon
1	cup frozen pearl onions, thawed	½	cup extra virgin olive oil
1	cup apple cider or fruit vinegar		

1. Combine the olives, mushrooms, onions, vinegar, chili flakes, lemon zest, and olive oil in a large jar with a lid and mix well.

2. Refrigerate and allow to marinate overnight. (I replenish the vegetables as I eat it, and I find that it tastes even better as time goes on and I add more ingredients.)

Smith Family Garden Pickles

MAKES 4 TO 5 QUARTS

Those of you who have gardens know how you sometimes have vegetables left at the end of season. I love to use them to make this relish, which is very similar to a Chicago Italian giardiniera. *This is perfect as a relish on its own, or served with your favorite hamburgers.*

1	cup sliced cucumbers	1	cup cauliflower florets
1	cup chopped red, green, or yellow bell peppers	1/4	cup chopped jalapeño peppers
1	cup sliced onions	1/4	cup canning or pickling salt
1	cup green beans, snapped in 1/2-inch lengths	1	gallon water
1	cup asparagus spears, cut into 1/2-inch lengths	2	cups apple cider vinegar
		1	cup sugar
1	cup sliced cabbage	1/4	cup pickling spices
1	cup sliced carrots	1	tablespoon celery seeds

1. In a large nonreactive stainless steel bowl, combine the cucumbers, peppers, onions, green beans, asparagus, cabbage, carrots, cauliflower, and jalapeño peppers. Combine the salt and water and pour over the vegetables, allowing it to sit overnight. Drain well.

2. Fill a large pot with water and bring to a boil over high heat.

3. Place the vegetables in the boiling water and blanch for 5 minutes. Drain and immediately transfer the vegetables to a bowl of ice water to crisp them. After 1 minute, drain well and transfer to hot sterilized canning jars.

4. In a nonreactive stainless steel saucepan, combine the vinegar, sugar, spices, and celery seeds. Place over medium-high heat and bring to a boil.

5. Once boiling, carefully pour over the vegetables in the sterilized jars, leaving 1/2 inch headspace. A canning funnel makes this step easy. Remove any air bubbles by tapping the sides of the jars.

6. Wipe the jar rims and tighten the lids on the jars.

7. Place the jars in a boiling water bath for 10 minutes. Make sure the water level is 1 inch above the jar tops.

8. Carefully remove the jars from the water with a jar lifter or sturdy tongs. Place them on a kitchen towel or wire rack. *Do not retighten screw bands.* Allow the jars to cool 12 to 24 hours before putting them away. Jar lids will pop as they cool. If the center of the lid is indented, the jar is sealed. If the jars do not seal, store them in the refrigerator.

Joannie Jones' Mother's Hot Pepper Jelly

MAKES 12 PINTS TO SHARE!

When this jelly became fashionable in Jasper, you would have thought it was some high fashion item. Every church lady in North Florida was making pints of it. I remember sitting by the pool one hot summer day, and Alice Jones served this to my mother and me. Don't forget the cream cheese—and Ritz Crackers will take you back.

8	green bell peppers	1½	cup white vinegar
8	red bell peppers	6	cups white sugar
4	jalapeños, minced or 2 tablespoons of red pepper flakes	4	packets dry pectin

1. Cut the peppers into chunks and combine them with the jalapeños in a food processor. (Use caution when handling jalapeños. Wash your hands well after handling them or use gloves.) Pulse the peppers until coarsely chopped.

2. Place the pepper puree in strainer and drain for 1 hour then transfer to paper towels to absorb more juice.

3. Combine the drained peppers, vinegar, sugar, and pectin in a saucepan over medium-high heat. Bring to a boil and boil steady for 1 minute.

4. Ladle into sterilized pint jars, leaving about ½ inch space from the top. Wipe the jar rims and adjust the lids, then place in a large pot and cover with boiling water. Water level must be 1 inch above the jars. Bring the water to a boil, then cover. Allow the jars to process in the boiling water bath for 10 minutes. Very carefully remove the jars with a jar lifter or sturdy tongs. They're hot!

5. Place the jars on a wire rack or dish towel. *Do not retighten screw bands.* Allow the jars to cool 12 to 24 hours before putting them away. Jar lids will pop as they cool. If the center of the lid is indented, the jar is sealed. If the jars do not seal, store in the refrigerator.

*Kind words can be short and easy to speak,
but their echoes are truly endless.*

—MOTHER THERESA

IN THE SOUTH, PUNCH IS A VERY COMMON DRINK served at all kinds of parties and receptions. Punches are a wonderful beverage for guests when prepared with fresh ingredients and nothing gets the pump primed like a few libations. When served "special," it is a polite way of saying it contains alcohol. You can give a drink to someone who is normally quiet and reserved, and all of a sudden they are talking up a storm. But remember—everything in moderation. Enjoy these special drinks!

Bloody Mary with Olive and Pepper Stir

MAKES 2 (8-OUNCE) DRINKS

These yummy brunch drinks are extra special because of their garnish. I love serving them to my friends and watching their faces light up. In season I use fresh tomatoes, but canned tomatoes make a really great drink, as well.

1	cup chopped tomatoes
2	stalks celery, coarsely chopped
1	green onion
¼	green bell pepper
1	cup tomato juice
	Dash of hot sauce
	Freshly ground black pepper to taste
	Dash of Worcestershire sauce

2 jiggers ice cold vodka

Garnish

Cayenne pepper to taste

Sea salt to taste

8	blue cheese–stuffed olives
8	sweet baby pickles
4	pieces pickled okra
4	cherry tomatoes

1. Combine the tomatoes, celery, green onion, bell pepper, tomato juice, hot sauce, black pepper, Worcestershire sauce, and vodka in a blender and puree.

2. Dip the glass rims in water, then in a mixture of cayenne and salt. Fill with ice and add the Bloody Mary mixture from the blender.

3. Complete the garnish by alternately skewing the olives, pickles, okra, and tomatoes. Place one skewer in each drink.

Sangria

MAKES 2 LARGE PITCHERS

I have been making sangria since the early days in my career at the Florida governor's mansion. Along the way I realized that my sangria was just as good as the sangria I had tasted in Spain. Here is a very simple and tasty recipe, great for a party and easy on the budget.

2	oranges, sliced	1	cup sugar
1	lemon, sliced	2	cups vodka
1	lime, sliced	1	cup Cointreau
1	apple, chopped	2	bottles red wine
1	pineapple, chopped	1	bottle sparkling water

1. In a large nonreactive pitcher or bowl, combine the oranges, lemon, lime, apple, pineapple, sugar, vodka, and Cointreau. Allow this mixture to marinate for a couple of hours in the refrigerator.

2. Add the red wine and stir well. Just before serving, splash with sparkling water. Serve over ice.

Electric Lemonade

MAKES 4 (6-OUNCE) DRINKS

This icy drink is one of the most famous drinks I have created during my career. It all started one day on Oprah's farm in Indiana. We had some nice lemons from California and lots of fresh mint. When you add the ice-cold vodka to the lemon juice with a little sugar, as my beloved Oprah says, "It can make you speak in tongues." To make this drink extraordinary, serve it in an ice-cold silver julep cup.

1	cup fresh squeezed lemon juice	2	cups ice
¼	cup sugar	1	cup vodka
½	cup fresh mint leaves	4	mint sprigs for garnish
1	cup sparkling mineral water	4	lemon slices for garnish
	Dash of ginger ale		Frozen vodka

1. Combine the lemon juice, sugar, mint, mineral water, ginger ale, and ice in a blender. Slowly blend until thick like a smoothie.

2. Remove four silver julep cups from the freezer and pour 1 jigger (¼ cup) of vodka in each cup.

3. Top with frozen lemonade mixture.

4. Drizzle a little frozen vodka over the top. Add a straw.

5. Garnish each cup with a fresh mint sprig and a slice of lemon.

Pomegranate Tequila Cocktail

Makes 2 (4-ounce) drinks

I invented this cocktail for a friend who had created his own line of tequila. As a bonus, a recent scientific finding tells us that pomegranate juice is healthy for us. This is one of my favorite holiday drinks to serve in my home kitchen.

½ cup pomegranate juice

¼ cup fresh orange juice

Juice of half a lime

2 jiggers or 6 tablespoons El Diamante del Ceilo Tequila, anejo

¼ cup ice

Dash of lemon-lime soda

Pomegranate seeds

Lime slices

1. In a cocktail shaker, combine the pomegranate, orange juice, and lime juice. Add the tequila and ice. Shake well.

2. Pour the mixture into a chilled martini glass and top with a dash of Fresca or lemon-lime soda.

3. Garnish with fresh pomegranate seeds and lime slices.

Iced Green Tea

Iced green tea is very refreshing and terrific on a hot summer day. Here is a drink with a kick that your guests will love.

4	cups green tea, brewed according to package directions	5	tablespoons sugar or artificial sweetener
1	cup fresh orange juice	1	jigger (3 tablespoons) rum
¼	cup lemon juice	1	jigger (3 tablespoons) vodka

1. Combine the tea, orange juice, lemon juice, sugar, rum, and vodka in a large pitcher. Mix well, stirring until the sugar dissolves.

2. Serve over ice.

CHAPTER 5

The Family Breakfast—Where Togetherness Begins

In the South breakfast is a very important meal. Southerners love it heavy and hearty, with a steaming cup of coffee within arm's reach. Breakfast is the perfect time to show our love. We can brighten a face or calm a fear with some simple food and a few kind words at the start of the day. Trust me, I have seen it work. I believe in the power of a nice cooked meal first thing in the morning.

Try it! Prepare a simple breakfast, sit down with your loved ones, and share. Talk to each other, pass the plates, give hugs, give kisses, and prepare yourself for the day ahead. Everyone knows how fast the world moves once we walk out that door. Enjoying breakfast—really enjoying the food and the company—can do wonders for everyone's peace of mind. When you are hungry you are never happy, so try not to skip this important meal. Get into the habit of spending quality time at breakfast—not just gulping down coffee and toast—and soon you will find that by the end of this morning ritual, you are standing and shouting to the world, "Good morning to ya!"

Besides being a great way to spend time with loved ones, for me breakfast is also the most satisfying meal of the day. The only thing I love better than cooking for people in the morning is taking them out for breakfast.

Eggs

Eggs are a wonderful part of any breakfast meal. They are beautiful to look at, for one thing, and their taste is so familiar and comforting. On the practical side, they are a great source of protein, and one of the most versatile cooking ingredients we have. Besides the obvious preparations—fried, coddled, poached, scrambled—they can also be used as a helper ingredient to enrich dishes.

We make all kinds of omelets at my house, and I have Pierre and his wife Rainey of Cheq Pierre to thank for that. They taught me the fine art of omelet making, and the French know it better than anyone. It was at Pierre and Rainey's darling café and pastry shop in Tallahassee where I learned to make omelets quickly for a hungry lunch crowd. It was quite challenging for me at the time, but I am grateful for the experience today because I often make these scrumptious treats at home, and for Ms. Winfrey, who simply adores them. The great thing about omelets is, you can use all kinds of ingredients in any combination—and half of the fun is coming up with new combinations—but really omelets are probably best when they are perfectly simple, with just some wonderful cheese inside.

Eggs are my favorite breakfast food. No matter how they are prepared, I love them. I suppose if I had to pick a favorite among my favorites it would be fried eggs served sunny-side up. My mother, Addie Mae, made them for me every morning when I was a boy. She fried them in bacon fat, just until they were set, and then served them with creamy hominy grits.

Grits

I've continued the grits tradition in Chicago. My family and friends adore them, and my dear friend Iris always asks me to make extra. She is from Missouri, where they love grits with butter and sugar, and when it is a grits morning at my house, Iris and I savor every grain. I special order mine from Charleston Cookery in Charleston, South Carolina. That is where my friend Mark Gray introduced me to Anson Mills stone-ground grits. They have changed my life!

There is something magical about any cooked grains in the morning. Another favorite is a warm bowl of Irish-cut oatmeal served with brown sugar and chopped dried fruits. These cereals take time to cook, but they are definitely worth the trouble. Make sure you save what you don't eat because the extras will make great fritters on another morning.

Casseroles

Preparing more than enough food is always a good idea, at least in my household. I know that if I invite four people over, usually eight show up! There is something gracious about having plenty of food on hand and being generous with it. I love feeding people, filling their stomachs, and bringing them joy at the table. It's all about the love, and there are many ways to express it. Food is a gift of love and I want to offer that gift to as many people as possible.

"Hots"

I've saved pancakes, waffles, biscuits, and fritters for last. Few things are better in the morning than eating these wonderful "hots" fresh out of the pan. Of course we know that we should eat these only occasionally. But when we do indulge in a good ol' southern breakfast, we should do it without reservation. We should think of it as a treat.

I like to make my "hots" from scratch, and serve them with crispy, thick-cut smoky bacon or homemade sausage. (Homemade sausage is a rare commodity these days, but it is worth looking for.) Let's not forget the maple syrup or my favorite, cane syrup. My great-grandparents, their children, and my father all loved biscuits bathed in it. Take those wonderful hot crusty biscuits straight from the oven, wash them with some butter, and cover them in luscious cane syrup. What could be better than that?

What about old-fashioned sausage gravy? That will certainly rock your world, but it is even less healthy than pancakes and syrup. Cook biscuits and gravy only once a year, but be ready for everyone to request it over and over again. Don't tell the neighbors you're making it, because they'll show up, too. But if you vow to start cooking more food than you think you'll need—as I do—then you'll be prepared.

My sincere wish is that you will prepare my breakfast dishes and make a habit of sharing them with your family and friends. Serve them with sweet words of love and a peck on the cheek. It's a hard world, and we work harder than ever to keep up with it. Start your day simply and together, because that is what keeps us grounded and focused on what is really important—our families and all the people we love.

THERE IS NO FOOD MORE COMPLETE THAN AN EGG.
I grew up on a farm and we ate eggs from chickens, ducks, turkeys, quails, guinea hens, and probably some birds I'm leaving out. The shells came in different sizes, but what was inside always had that luscious fresh egg taste. I love the way eggs enrich dishes. And of course I love them for breakfast either simply fried or sprinkled with chorizo and a little queso fresco cheese.

One of the simplest and most elegant egg dishes is the classic omelet. My dear friends Rainey and Pierre taught me how to make this fine dish. First, you must get a really great nonstick omelet pan. Don't spend a lot of money because if you scratch it you can just throw it away and get a new one. Nothing upsets me more than an omelet that sticks to the pan. If that happens, simply throw cheese on top and call it scrambled eggs.

Open-Faced Eggs

MAKES 1 SERVING

As a child I loved eating eggs sunny-side up. I know that some people don't enjoy them with soft yolks, so in that case just break the yolk and cook it with the sausage and cheese. This is still a great breakfast meal. Occasionally I also put a piece of toast under my eggs and serve them like an open-faced sandwich. You can even cut out a circle in the bread and break the egg into the cutout and fry it like that. The English call it "Toad in the Hole."

2 eggs

4 ounces chorizo sausage, fried crisp and drained well

1 tablespoon queso fresco or Farmer's cheese, crumbled

1 tablespoon chopped fresh cilantro

Salt and freshly ground pepper to taste

1. Place a nonstick lightly greased skillet over medium heat.

2. Break the eggs into the skillet.

3. Watching the heat, carefully cook the eggs sunny-side up.

4. Sprinkle with the sausage, cheese, and cilantro while the eggs are not yet set.

5. Sprinkle with freshly ground pepper and a light amount of salt. I like to serve this with creamy stone-ground grits (see recipe on page 68).

Open-Faced Eggs Verde

MAKES 1 SERVING

I love eggs with asparagus and zucchini. Sprinkle on some Parmesan cheese, and add sea salt and freshly ground pepper to top it off! Also, try adding Salsa Verde (see recipe on page 271) or Salsa Roja to your eggs, too.

2	eggs	2	tablespoons Parmesan cheese
1	stalk asparagus, blanched and cut into 4 pieces		Salt and fresh ground pepper to taste
½	small zucchini, blanched and cut into 4 sticks		Thinly sliced prosciutto (optional)

1. Break the eggs into a nonstick, greased skillet, placed over medium heat.

2. Slowly fry the eggs. Before they are set, scatter the vegetables around them, then sprinkle with the Parmesan cheese.

3. Season with salt and pepper. Cook until desired doneness and serve with toast. Add some prosciutto on top before serving if desired.

Mushroom and Goat Cheese Omelet

MAKES 1 OMELET

Mushrooms have been used in omelets for a long time, but adding goat cheese makes a familiar dish new and exciting. Goat cheese also gives an omelet a special creaminess.

1½ tablespoons olive oil

1 tablespoon butter

¼ cup diced onion

½ clove garlic, minced

4 white button mushrooms, thinly sliced

3 eggs

¼ cup half-and-half

⅛ teaspoon salt

Freshly ground black pepper to taste

3 tablespoons goat cheese, crumbled

1. Heat the olive oil and butter in a nonstick sauté pan over medium-high heat. When hot, add the onion and garlic. Cook for 1 to 2 minutes.

2. Add the mushrooms and cook for 1 to 2 minutes. Reduce the heat to medium. In a bowl beat the eggs, half-and-half, salt, and pepper.

3. Add the eggs to the pan and stir constantly with a rubber spatula. Cook until the center of the eggs is just a little runny. Place the goat cheese in a row down the center. Fold the omelet over and transfer to a serving plate. It will finish cooking and be done by the time it gets to the table. This is known as "carry-over cooking."

Spinach, Olive, and Feta Omelet

MAKES 1 OMELET

My dear, dear friend Connie Pikalus, whose family immigrated to the United States from Greece, taught me about premium feta. It is made in many countries besides Greece and, believe me, there is a huge difference in quality. When selecting feta for this omelet, choose one that is not too salty. I even wash a little of the brine off the olives, too. Combining these already-salty flavors with spinach makes a perfect omelet.

1	tablespoon olive oil	3	eggs
1	tablespoon butter	1	sprig rosemary, chopped
$\frac{1}{2}$	clove garlic, minced	$\frac{1}{4}$	cup half-and-half
4	cherry tomatoes, halved	$\frac{1}{2}$	pinch salt
4	ounces (1 cup) baby spinach	$\frac{1}{4}$	teaspoon black pepper
4	to 6 pitted black olives, sliced	$\frac{1}{4}$	cup feta cheese, crumbled

1. Place a nonstick sauté pan over medium-high heat. Add the olive oil and butter. When the butter is melted, add the garlic and halved tomatoes. Cook for 1 to 2 minutes.

2. Add the baby spinach and olives and cook for 1 to 2 minutes more, or until all of the spinach is wilted, then reduce the heat to medium.

3. Beat the eggs, rosemary, half-and-half, salt, and pepper and pour into the pan. Stir constantly so that the eggs do not brown. When the center is just a little soft, crumble the feta cheese all around the omelet. Fold onto the plate and serve.

Basil and Tomato Omelet

In late summer, when tomatoes are everywhere and basil is exceptionally fragrant, this is the perfect brunch or lunch meal. I love this with an arugula salad on the side and an iced coffee.

1	tablespoon butter	¼	cup freshly grated Parmesan cheese (set aside 1 tablespoon for garnish)
1½	tablespoons olive oil		
½	clove garlic, minced	¼	cup half-and-half
2	cherry tomatoes, halved	1	pinch salt
3	eggs	¼	teaspoon freshly ground black pepper

1. Heat the butter and olive oil in a nonstick sauté pan over medium-high heat. When hot add the garlic and halved tomatoes and cook for 1 to 2 minutes.

2. Turn the heat down to medium, then beat the eggs, Parmesan cheese, half-and-half, and salt and pepper together in a medium bowl.

3. Pour into the pan and stir constantly, not letting the eggs brown. The center of the omelet should be a little runny.

4. Fold the omelet over and transfer to a serving plate. Sprinkle the remaining Parmesan cheese on top.

Caramelized Onion, Arugula, and Parmesan Cheese Omelet

MAKES 1 OMELET

Most people who hate onions hate them because they are undercooked. There is only one onion that tastes good undercooked and even better raw, and that is a Vidalia onion. Vidalias are a real find when they are in season. When you're using simple white onions, caramelize them (see recipe on page 258) or cook them until they are translucent. You can cook them ahead and keep them in your refrigerator for later use. The arugula adds a nice, sharp fresh flavor.

1 tablespoon olive oil	½ cup freshly grated Parmesan cheese (set 1 tablespoon aside for garnish)
1 tablespoon butter	
⅓ cup caramelized onions	¼ teaspoon freshly ground black pepper
½ clove garlic, minced	
¼ cup arugula	Dash of salt
3 eggs	

1. Heat the olive oil and butter in a nonstick sauté pan over high heat. When hot add the caramelized onions, garlic, and arugula and sauté for about 1 minute or until the greens have wilted. Reduce the heat to medium.

2. Beat the eggs, Parmesan cheese, pepper, and salt together and then pour the mixture into the sauté pan, stirring constantly. When the center of the eggs is just a little soft, fold onto a serving plate and sprinkle the remaining Parmesan cheese on top.

*The best portion of a good man's life
is his little nameless unremembered
acts of kindness and of love.*
—WILLIAM WORDSWORTH

GRITS ARE AN INSTITUTION IN THE SOUTH, AND considered to be the regional dish. Most people who are not familiar with the South have strange ideas about our beloved grits. Trust me, though, when they are perfectly cooked, they are simply the best. First, you have to find quality grits. I love Anson Mills stone-ground grits, and I can also find terrific grits at Bradley's Country Store near my home in Florida. These take longer to cook but have a better texture and taste.

Creamy Grits

The secret to wonderful creamy grits is to cook them on low heat and use milk and water. You can put them in a slow cooker overnight and they are perfect for breakfast—especially convenient if you are hosting a big breakfast crowd.

1 cup stone-ground grits, soaked in water overnight	4 tablespoons unsalted butter or cream cheese
2 cups water	Salt and freshly ground black pepper to taste
2 cups milk	

1. In a heavy pot add the soaked grits, water, milk, butter, salt, and pepper and bring to a boil.

2. Reduce the heat, cover, and simmer. Cook 25 minutes, stirring occasionally. Serve immediately.

Baked Cheese Grits

MAKES 4 SERVINGS

*For those folks who can't stand basic grits, these are wonderful. We enjoy them regularly in the South, especially with fried fish and smothered shrimp. **Yummy!** The key to making this recipe taste good is high-quality cheddar cheese. We also add the "holy trinity"—onion, celery, and green pepper—to this dish, which my good friend Ben Baldwin affectionately calls "Nassau Grits."*

1	Creamy Grits recipe (see recipe on page 68)	1	clove garlic, minced
1	teaspoon bacon grease or olive oil	1	cup shredded sharp cheddar cheese or Pepper Jack cheese
1	onion, chopped	2	egg yolks, beaten
1	bell pepper, chopped	2	egg whites, beaten
1	stalk celery, chopped		

1. Preheat the oven to 350 degrees. Grease a 2-quart casserole dish.

2. In a large skillet over medium-high heat, melt the bacon grease. When hot, add the onion, bell pepper, celery, and garlic. Sauté until the onions are translucent.

3. Stir the sautéed vegetables and the cheese into the grits.

4. Carefully stir the beaten yolks into the grits.

5. Gently fold the beaten egg whites into the grits and pour the mixture into the prepared casserole dish.

6. Bake 30 to 40 minutes. Serve immediately.

IN FLORIDA AT THE GOVERNOR'S MANSION, MY

"Tallahassee lassie," Nella Schomburger, taught me so much about cooking for casts of thousands. One thing I'll always be grateful for is her turning me on to the fine art of making beautiful breakfast casseroles. These one-dish wonders are incredibly easy to prepare, and sure make one's life easier in the early morning. Coming out of culinary school you have eggs Benedict and mimosa cocktails on the brain. But a perfectly prepared breakfast casserole with the right ingredients, including organic eggs—try them once and you'll never be able to eat a regular egg again!—can rival any fancy-looking food. There's nothing better for a large breakfast crowd than a casserole, a simple truth I learned shortly after I began cooking at the governor's mansion.

Asparagus with Manchego Cheese

Asparagus and Manchego cheese have become such a welcome part of my cooking repertoire that they inspire me to create new recipes using them. I love asparagus. My mother began feeding me pieces of Del Monte asparagus when I was just a babe. Many years later when I visited Spain, I discovered Manchego cheese. They form a perfect marriage of flavor.

½ loaf French bread, cut in small cubes

1 tablespoon extra virgin olive oil

1 onion, diced

1 pint (2 cups) halved cherry or grape tomatoes

1 bunch asparagus, cut in ½-inch pieces on the bias (3½ cups)

8 eggs

1 cup milk

½ cup freshly grated Parmesan cheese

1 teaspoon kosher salt

Freshly ground black pepper to taste

1 cup shredded manchego cheese

1. Preheat the oven to 350 degrees.

2. Place the French bread cubes in a lightly greased 13 x 9-inch baking dish.

3. Place the extra virgin olive oil in a sauté pan over medium heat. Add the onion and cook until translucent, 3 to 4 minutes.

4. Add the tomatoes and asparagus. Cook another 2 minutes, and then pour over the bread cubes in the casserole dish.

5. Whip the eggs, milk, Parmesan cheese, salt, and black pepper. Pour on top of the vegetable mixture. Sprinkle the manchego cheese evenly over the top.

6. Bake for 40 to 45 minutes. Serve immediately.

Breakfast Casserole with Ciabatta

MAKES 6 LARGE SERVINGS

Italian bacon, fresh spinach, and Parmesan cheese—a wonderful combination in the early morning or for a brunch or luncheon.

1½ loaves Ciabatta bread, cut in medium cubes

5   ounces pancetta, chopped

1   whole shallot, minced

2   cloves garlic, minced

8   ounces (2 cups) baby spinach

8   eggs

2   sprigs fresh rosemary, chopped

2   sprigs fresh thyme, chopped

1½ cups freshly grated Parmesan cheese

1¼ cups milk

1   teaspoon kosher salt

    Freshly ground black pepper to taste

1. Preheat the oven to 350 degrees.

2. Place the bread cubes in a lightly greased 13 x 9-inch baking dish.

3. Cook the diced pancetta in a large sauté pan over medium-low heat for 3 or 4 minutes to render the fat. Remove all but 1 tablespoon of the fat from the pan.

4. Add the shallots and garlic, and cook for 2 or 3 minutes. Add the baby spinach and cook until all of the spinach has wilted, then add it to the casserole dish over the bread.

5. Whip the eggs and then add the chopped herbs, Parmesan cheese, milk, salt, and black pepper.

6. Pour into the casserole dish over the pancetta mixture and bake for 40 to 45 minutes. Serve immediately.

Brioche Casserole

I love a breakfast casserole. These fabulous one-dish, early-morning wonders will save you time. Better yet, they taste great. My beloved friend Nella Schomburger taught me the fine art of preparing these dishes. (See photo on page 70.)

1 loaf brioche, cut in medium cubes	¼ cup chopped fresh parsley
1 cup shredded mild cheddar cheese	8 eggs, whipped
½ cup shredded Monterey Jack cheese	1 cup milk
	1 teaspoon kosher salt
	Freshly ground black pepper to taste

1. Preheat the oven to 350 degrees.

2. Place the brioche cubes in a lightly greased 13 x 9-inch casserole dish. Set a couple of tablespoons of both cheeses to the side for the top of the casserole.

3. Combine the parsley with the eggs. Add the remaining cheese, milk, salt, and pepper and stir to mix well.

4. Pour into the prepared baking dish and top with the reserved cheese.

5. Bake for 40 to 45 minutes. Check the center of the casserole with a toothpick or paring knife. If the casserole is done, it will come out clean. Serve immediately.

*I've always believed that people who have lived
close to the earth have an appreciation for life,
and a humbleness about them.*
—ART SMITH

hotcakes, biscuits, and fritters

IN MY BELOVED SOUTH, PANCAKES AND HOTCAKES are popular breakfast items. I grew up attending Lions Club pancake suppers. At home my mother, Addie Mae, would make them for my brother Gene and me sometimes for supper. Remember, great cakes come from batter that has not been overbeaten. Also, I only use Martha White self-rising flour for my cakes. And don't forget the cane syrup!

Sour Cream Pancakes

What is breakfast without pancakes? These remind me of my childhood. I love them early in the morning and also for supper. There is nothing like a few of these with the best honey and some wonderful butter. Sour cream makes very tender pancakes and also gives them a wonderful tang.

2 cups self-rising flour	1 teaspoon pure vanilla extract
2 tablespoons sugar	1 cup sour cream
1 large egg, beaten	1 cup buttermilk
2 tablespoons unsalted butter, melted	Vegetable oil
	Honey or maple syrup

1. Preheat the oven to 200 degrees to keep the pancakes warm as you make them.

2. Sift the flour and sugar together in a bowl.

3. In another bowl place the beaten egg, melted butter, vanilla, sour cream, and buttermilk. Beat this mixture well.

4. Without overmixing, combine the wet and the dry ingredients. Lumps are okay; they will cook off in the heat. You may wish to thin down the batter with a little water or milk.

5. Brush a nonstick pan or griddle with vegetable oil and place over medium heat. Using a ladle, pour the desired amount of batter onto the hot griddle.

6. When the pancakes begin to bubble, flip to cook the other side. Cook the pancakes for about 2 minutes per side.

7. Place the pancakes on a sheet pan and keep them warm in the oven. Serve with honey or maple syrup.

Granola Pancakes

I first tasted these wonderful cakes at the Santa Barbara Beach Club. If you are ever in that part of California, there is nothing better than sitting on the beach eating these wonderful hot cakes while people watching. Sprinkling granola on one side gives the cakes a crunchy texture, which makes them even more enjoyable. (See photo on page 78.)

1	Sour Cream Pancakes recipe (see recipe on page 80)	2	cups granola

1. Make batter according to the Sour Cream Pancakes recipe.

2. Brush a nonstick pan or griddle with vegetable oil and place over medium heat. Using a ladle, pour the desired amount of batter onto the griddle and sprinkle with granola.

3. When the pancakes begin to bubble, flip to cook the other side. Cook the pancakes for about 2 minutes per side.

4. Place pancakes on a sheet pan and keep them warm in the oven. Serve with honey or maple syrup.

Farm-Baked Apple Pancakes

MAKES 12 PANCAKES

These wonderful cakes bring back memories of Oprah's farm in Indiana. I loved going next door to Williams Orchards and buying apples to make these wonderful cakes for weekend guests.

1 Sour Cream Pancakes recipe (see recipe on page 80)	¼ teaspoon ground cinnamon
½ cup apple juice	2 green or red apples, peeled and sliced into thin wedges
¼ cup sugar	

1. Make batter according to the Sour Cream Pancake recipe.

2. Preheat the oven to 400 degrees.

3. Place a sauté pan over medium heat. When hot, add the apple juice, sugar, and cinnamon to the sauté pan and slowly reduce until the liquid thickens. Transfer to a bowl and set aside.

4. Reheat the sauté pan after spraying it with nonstick spray, and fan out the apples starting from the middle of the pan. Go around the sauté pan clockwise. Cook for 2 to 4 minutes.

5. Add the pancake batter to cover the apples. Try not to overfill the pan, just enough to thinly cover the apples.

6. Place the pan on the top rack of the preheated oven and bake for 2 minutes. The color of the top of the pancake should be light brown.

7. Remove the pan from the oven and trace around the edges with a rubber spatula.

8. Place a plate over the pan and flip. The pancake should pop right out. Serve with reserved apple syrup.

Corn Fritters

MAKES 1 DOZEN FRITTERS

Corn fritters are a very popular batter cake in the heartland of America. You will find these cakes wherever corn is grown. I love them fried in bacon fat—so delicious, but hard on the heart. I always serve them with crispy bacon because the sweetness of the corn next to the saltiness of the bacon is the best.

	Canola Oil	$1\frac{1}{2}$	cups self-rising flour
2	large eggs, beaten	1	teaspoon sugar
$1\frac{1}{2}$	cups buttermilk		Butter
	Salt and pepper		Maple syrup
1	(16-ounce) can cream-style corn or 4 ears fresh corn, cut off the cob		

1. In a nonstick skillet, add enough canola oil until it is about $\frac{1}{4}$-inch deep. Place over medium heat.

2. Meanwhile, in a large bowl combine the eggs, buttermilk, salt, pepper, and corn. Mix well.

3. Sift the flour into the bowl and then add the sugar. Mix well.

4. Test the heat of the skillet with a little batter. If the batter sizzles, it's ready. Drop 3 tablespoons of batter into the hot oil, and fry 2 to 3 minutes per side.

5. Remove and place on paper towels to absorb the excess oil. Serve with butter and maple syrup.

Multigrain Breakfast Cereal

This hot cereal is a favorite of many people in my life who want something healthy and warm for breakfast. On those cold Chicago mornings, this really hits the spot.

¼ cup steel cut oats

¼ cup pearl barley

¼ cup wheat berries

2 tablespoons flax seed

Pinch of salt

3 cups water, or as needed

1. In a heavy saucepan add grains, water, and a pinch of salt. Cook for 1 hour, or until the grains are tender. When grains are done, stir in flax seeds, and sweeten with desired sweetener. Add extra milk if needed.

NOTE: I cook the grains the day before and refrigerate. The next morning I just add milk or water to soften them, heat them in the microwave, and enjoy.

Baking Powder Biscuits and Sausage Gravy

In many parts of our country, especially in the heartland, this is a very popular dish. It is also a dish that has been totally ruined at times. You must make fresh baking powder biscuits—none of that store bought stuff—a good cast-iron skillet, and don't forget the "holy trinity" (a must in the South) of onion, celery, and green pepper. I always begin my dishes with that, plus a little garlic. My dear friend and sous chef, Rey Villalobos, whose family is from Mexico, now adds chiles to my recipe, and I love the extra spice. Use jalapeño or serrano chiles, but be careful. Just a little heat creates a big taste.

Biscuits

2 cups self-rising flour

1 tablespoon sugar

2 tablespoons unsalted butter, cold

2 tablespoons vegetable shortening, cold

¾ cup buttermilk

Gravy

1 pound Italian sausage, crumbled

1 onion, chopped

1 stalk celery, chopped

1 clove garlic, minced

2 tablespoons flour

½ cup chicken broth

1 cup 2% milk

2 tablespoons heavy cream

Salt and freshly ground black pepper to taste

1. **For the biscuits,** in a food processor, add the flour, sugar, butter, and shortening. Pulse the ingredients until they resemble coarse meal.

2. Gradually add the buttermilk, pulsing until you have dough. Remove and chill 15 minutes. Preheat the oven to 425 degrees.

3. On a lightly floured surface, roll the biscuits out to ¹/₂-inch thickness and 4 inches in diameter. Cut into 2-inch rounds.

4. Place on a heavy sheet pan and bake in a preheated oven until brown, about 12 minutes.

5. Remove from the oven and split in half and/or serve whole with gravy on the side.

6. **For gravy,** in a cast-iron skillet, fry the sausage over medium-high heat until brown, then add the onions, celery, and garlic and cook until the onions are translucent.

7. Add the flour and cook until lightly browned.

8. Gradually stir in the chicken broth until it begins to thicken.

9. Remove from the heat and add the milk and cream. Do not boil! Season with salt and pepper. Serve immediately.

NOTE: I use southern self-rising flour and buttermilk, and I like to bake my biscuits in a preheated skillet to give them a crusty bottom.

CHAPTER 6

Lunch—Love in the Afternoon

In my beloved South, lunch is always called dinner, a charming expression used to indicate the midday meal. Historically, dinner (a.k.a. lunch) was a meal crucial to the success of people who toiled at manual labor. Dinner was a meal that helped these hard-working folks restore their strength and fortified them for the rest of their demanding day.

It was also a show of appreciation. In the old days of the South, dinner was an event—a big meal that broke up the day—and was always larger than supper, the evening meal. I am amazed at how hard the women of the rural South worked to feed their hardworking husbands and sons. The women woke up early in the morning and fired up wood-burning potbelly stoves. They heated large skillets on the stoves and prepared flaky biscuits and creamy gravy. Sometimes the women filled those biscuits with a sliver of country ham or homemade preserves and then wrapped them in handkerchiefs for the men's midmorning snack in the fields. This hearty morning fare held folks until the noon hour, when heaping platters of fried chicken and pork chops and endless fresh vegetable sides would appear. The men in the fields needed heavy food so they could continue their physically demanding work.

Hominy Corn

One pioneer dish that was very popular was hominy corn. To make it, my ancestors dried corn in towering corncribs before placing it in large cast-iron kettles filled with lye. The corn was soaked in the heated lye water bath, and eventually the husks fell away leaving only beautiful white kernels all plump and tender. After several fresh-water baths to rinse off the lye, the kernels could be transformed into our traditional dish. Hominy corn, often cooked in bacon drippings, became a staple for our family, and my father still requests it to this very day.

Tribute to Great-Grandmother Margaret

We can all relate a person to a food, can't we? Aren't there foods in our lives that we can't think of without thinking of the person who loves them so well, or cooks them so well, or first introduced them to us? There are also those special people who bring everyone together. In my family, that was my great-grandmother. With the help of her daughters, my great-grandmother Margaret, the matriarch of the Smith family, prepared enormous meals for those who worked on our farm. I think dinner became special to us because of the love and passion she had for our farm, a spirit she passed on to all of us.

She was an amazing woman who endured more adversity than one person should have to endure. Besides the day-to-day hardship of rural life and the fickleness of farming, she also sent a son off to war in the foreign land of her ancestors, Germany; nursed her family through a yellow fever epidemic; and managed to feed and house them all during the Great Depression. Medicine is nice when it is available and affordable, and money usually makes things easier, but my great-grandmother realized there was an even simpler key to survival and happiness. Her motto said it all: "When you have food, all is okay."

These days we have grown accustomed to having everything at our fingertips. In the midst of our streamlined daily routines we sometimes forget what our ancestors went through to preserve our families. Many of them were lucky just to have a roof over their heads and food on the table.

Tribute to My Mother—Addie Mae

In the 1960s my mother, Addie Mae, was a beautiful woman (as she still is today) who worked very hard. Addie Mae is one of the most loved ladies in Jasper. A modern-day version of my great-grandmother, she is a woman of great resolve who has never hesitated to help others in need while still taking good care of her own family. As a daughter of the Depression, she too believes in the importance of food. When we talk on the phone and I tell her which movie star or celebrity I have cooked for most recently, she tells me how nice that is and then immediately asks if I'm eating right and taking care of myself. Always a mom!

When my brother, Gene, and I were boys, my mother always sent us to school with lunchboxes packed with goodness. I still remember those wonderful little packages of love she would tuck away in those colorful boxes. There was no trading lunch with schoolmates for Gene and me because we knew nothing could top what our mother had waiting for us! There were no ready-made lunches in those days, and even if there had been, my mother would have scoffed at them. She believed in wholesome sandwiches made with real turkey and baked ham, and real fruit juice or milk for a drink.

Children and Lunch

I am saddened at how our schoolchildren eat these days. In Chicago I constantly see snack packages of all kinds littering sidewalks and clinging to fences. Our children are eating on the go, and they are eating unnatural food for breakfast, lunch, and as afternoon snacks. I hope that at least they are getting a good meal at home in the evening. I have to admit that my mother sometimes gave Gene and me small baggies of chips in those glorious lunches of yesteryear, but chips were a treat to us, and never taken for granted.

Many mothers who read my articles in *O* or my monthly column on Oprah.com write and ask my advice on how to get their children to eat better. I always say, "Just allow your children to tell you what they want to eat and come to compromises." In other words, say, "Okay, dear, you can have your treats, but I want you to try these other foods, too." I believe that when you give kids a choice and treat them as grown-ups or emerging adults, you will begin to see a difference in their attitude about food.

Soups, Salads, and Sandwiches

How about a healthy turkey burger served on multigrain bread for lunch? My family can't get enough of those. Another suggestion is a nice chopped salad. Before you shoot that idea down, trust me for a second. I know there are people out there with kids—and adults—in their lives who simply don't do vegetables. Cut up some grilled chicken, turkey, shrimp, or cheese in the salad and they won't even realize they're eating vegetables.

Ms. Winfrey loves a nice chopped salad for lunch, and to make lunch more complete she adds a bowl of soup. Soup is one of my favorite things to make, even if it is something as simple as a turkey chili, bean soup, or a pureed primavera. The great thing is that soup is another way for us to sneak vegetables into those mouths that usually adhere to a "no vegetable" policy. And if you haven't had soup for a while, you may have forgotten how good it makes you feel inside.

Times have changed since my great-grandmother's days. We live more comfortably now and more predictably, and we no longer need to eat heavy, sustaining food. One thing has not changed, though, and that is the message sent by a wholesome midday meal. Whether it is packed lovingly in a box or served at home, it always says, *I love you.*

SOUP IS MY ABSOLUTE FAVORITE MEAL. I MAKE ALL kinds of soups, and friends request them again and again. Many people forget that a great soup and salad is a perfect meal. Countless people have asked me about the secret behind the weight loss of my famous clients. It's no secret—it's soup. And don't forget the green salad. Trust me, it will set you free!

Clam Chowder

I love to make this for dinner for my clients. Yes, it has cream, but have it and a big salad and it will set you free. What a wonderful satisfying meal! Enjoy it on those cold dark winter evenings.

2   ounces country ham or bacon, chopped

1   Vidalia onion, chopped

1   cup chopped celery

2   cloves garlic, minced

½   tablespoon all-purpose flour

2   cups bottled clam broth

2   medium potatoes, peeled and cubed

1   teaspoon Old Bay Seasoning

1   cup whipping cream

2   cups fresh shucked clams

    Sherry wine

1. Fry the ham in a Dutch oven over medium heat until crispy. Remove the ham and add the onion, celery, and garlic. Add the flour and cook for about 2 minutes. Add clam broth, potatoes, Old Bay, and whipping cream and cook for 5 minutes. Bring to a simmer and add the clams. Cook for 2 minutes and remove from the heat. A little Sherry splashed on top is wonderful.

*In our ever changing world, if we are lucky,
family is one thing that holds constant.*
—ART SMITH

Puree of Roasted Pumpkin and Butternut Squash Soup

MAKES 4 SERVINGS

Squash is one of those vegetables that is usually greeted with either a smile or a frown. I love squash, and as a little kid my mother made the best squash casserole east of the Suwannee River. In this recipe we combine pumpkin with squash to make a superb soup. So, all you folks who do not like squash—beware. This soup will change your mind.

1	medium pumpkin (about 2½ pounds), quartered and seeded	1	to 2 carrots, diced to make ½ cup
2	butternut squash (about ½ pound each), quartered and seeded	2	cloves garlic, chopped
		½	teaspoon ground cinnamon
3	tablespoons olive oil, divided	¼	teaspoon star anise
2	onions, diced to make 1 cup	¼	teaspoon nutmeg
2	stalks celery, diced to make ½ cup	1½	quarts vegetable stock
			Salt and freshly ground black pepper to taste

1. Preheat the oven to 350 degrees. Drizzle the pumpkin and squash with 1 tablespoon olive oil. Rub them completely, coating all sides. Then season with salt and pepper. On a sheet pan lined with parchment paper, place in the oven and roast until tender, about 45 to 55 minutes.

2. In a stockpot, heat the remaining olive oil over medium-high heat and add the onions, celery, carrots, and garlic. Sauté for 6 to 8 minutes. Then add the spices and cook for 2 to 4 minutes.

3. Remove the squash and pumpkin from the oven. Check them with a paring knife—there should be no resistance. Set aside and let cool.

4. When cooled, remove the skin and add the "meat" to the pot with the rest of the ingredients. Add the stock, bring to a boil for 5 minutes, and then reduce to a simmer for 10 minutes.

5. Puree all of the soup with an emersion blender, or allow the soup to cool slightly and puree in a standard blender. This should give the soup a nice consistency.

6. Season with salt and pepper and serve hot.

Puree of Wild Mushroom Soup

This is probably one of the fanciest recipes in my book, but it is a fabulous soup that I make time and time again. The dried mushrooms give the soup its wonderful flavor. If you have never used dried mushrooms, remember that they need to be hydrated in warm water and washed a couple of times. They can be very sandy, and that is one texture you do not want in your food. Enjoy!

2 tablespoons dried porcini mushrooms	3 tablespoons olive oil
2 tablespoons dried chanterelle mushrooms	2 onions, diced to make 1 cup
2 tablespoons dried cremini mushrooms	2 to 3 stalks celery, diced to make ½ cup
½ cup fresh chanterelle mushrooms, sliced	1 to 2 carrots, diced to make ½ cup
½ cup button mushrooms, sliced	2 cloves garlic, chopped
3 ounces baby portobellos, sliced	1½ quarts chicken or vegetable stock
3 ounces shiitake mushrooms, sliced	Salt and freshly ground black pepper to taste

1. Place the dried mushrooms in hot water and set aside to rehydrate for 15 to 20 minutes.

2. Meanwhile, heat the olive oil in a large stockpot over medium-high heat. When hot, add the onions, celery, carrots, and garlic and sauté for about 6 to 8 minutes until the onions are translucent and the vegetables are tender.

3. Add the fresh mushrooms and cook for 4 to 6 more minutes. Remove the dried mushrooms from the liquid and add to the pot.

4. Add the stock and bring it to a boil for 5 minutes, then reduce the heat and bring it to a simmer for 10 minutes.

5. Remove from the heat. Puree all of the soup with an emersion blender, or allow the soup to cool slightly and puree in a standard blender. This should give the soup a nice consistency without adding any kind of thickener. Serve immediately.

Gazpacho

I love Spain, and I especially love spending time in Barcelona. When I'm there I enjoy countless bowls of gazpacho. In Florida we try to reconnect to our heritage, and gazpacho comes in two colors: white and red. They are both delicious and they're a terrific way for you to get your vegetables. When you make gazpacho you can grind your vegetables until they are smooth, or leave them a little chunky. Either way it's a great healthful soup.

¼ sweet onion, chopped

4 cups chopped tomatoes (about 8 tomatoes)

1 large cucumber, chopped

2 cloves garlic, minced

¼ cup olive oil

1 bell pepper, seeded and chopped

1 jalapeño pepper, seeded and chopped

Salt and freshly ground black pepper to taste

6 cups tomato juice

1 cup chopped fresh cilantro (reserve some for garnish)

¼ cup chopped fresh basil

1. Combine the onion, tomatoes, cucumber, garlic, oil, bell pepper, jalapeño, and salt and pepper in a large bowl. Cover and refrigerate overnight.

2. Place the mixture in a blender, add the tomato juice, cilantro, and basil, and puree. Consistency should be a medium thickness, almost like applesauce.

3. When everything is pureed to your liking, garnish with some cilantro and serve.

Tomato Fennel Soup

MAKES 4 SERVINGS

Hot soup is a wonderful meal in itself or a great way to begin dinner on a cold day. This is one of my favorite soups and it's very simple to make.

2	tablespoons olive oil	1	cup chicken broth
½	onion, chopped	2	tablespoons chopped fresh basil
1	stalk celery, chopped	2	tablespoons chopped fresh parsley
1	clove garlic, minced		
1	fennel bulb, chopped		Salt and freshly ground black pepper to taste
1	(14.5-ounce) can diced tomatoes, undrained		

1. In a large saucepan, heat the olive oil over medium-high heat. When hot, add the onion, celery, garlic, and fennel. Cook until the vegetables are tender, about 4 minutes.

2. Add the tomatoes and chicken broth and simmer 3 to 4 minutes.

3. Remove from the heat and add the basil and parsley. Puree the soup with an emersion blender or cool slightly and puree in a standard blender.

4. Season with salt and pepper. Serve hot.

Pureed Artichoke Soup

MAKES 4 SERVINGS

This is a simple soup I created one day for Ms. Winfrey. I always joke about how my boss's middle name should be "Artichoke." She adores artichokes and this is a fabulous soup, with the wonderful taste of that delectable thistle vegetable.

2	tablespoons olive oil	4	artichoke hearts
1	onion, chopped	2	cups chicken broth
1	stalk celery, chopped		Salt and freshly ground pepper to taste
1	clove garlic, minced		
1	Yukon gold potato, peeled and cubed		

1. Heat the olive oil in a large saucepan over medium-high heat. Add the onion, celery, garlic, potato, and artichoke hearts. Cook until the vegetables are tender, about 5 minutes.

2. Add the chicken broth and simmer for 5 minutes. Remove from the heat and then puree with an emersion blender or cool slightly and puree with a standard blender until smooth.

3. Season with salt and freshly ground pepper. Serve hot.

Garden Pea and Fresh Mint Soup

MAKES 4 SERVINGS

This is a favorite summer soup of mine, served cold or slightly warm. Even people who don't like peas love it!

2	tablespoons olive oil	2	cups chicken broth
1	onion, chopped	1	tablespoon lemon juice
1	stalk celery, chopped	1	cup fresh mint leaves
1	clove garlic, minced	½	cup plain yogurt
1	(10-ounce) package frozen green peas		Salt and freshly ground pepper to taste

1. Heat the olive oil in a large saucepan over medium-high heat. Add the onion, celery, and garlic and cook until tender, about 4 minutes.

2. Add the peas and chicken broth and bring to a simmer.

3. Remove from the heat and add the lemon juice and mint leaves. Puree with an emersion blender or cool slightly and puree in a standard blender.

4. Add the yogurt and puree again to mix. Chill well and season with salt and pepper before serving.

Turkey Chili

My favorite thing to do is shop, and one day while shopping I made a great discovery—Darn Good Chili Mix. Following the lead of my mother, I use it to "doctor up" my chili recipe. There are many delicious chilis, but this one seems to always win folks over. When I prepare it for friends, I make extra to store in the freezer. Don't forget to do the same for yourself before it's all gone. It's that good!

2	tablespoons olive oil		2	stalks celery, chopped
2	pounds ground turkey (made from both white and dark meat)		½	green bell pepper, chopped
			½	red bell pepper, chopped
1	pound Italian turkey sausage, casings removed		2	cloves garlic, minced
			1	(16-ounce) can stewed tomatoes, undrained
1	tablespoon smoked paprika			
2	tablespoons ground Chile Molido or ground red pepper (see pantry)		1	package chili seasoning (see pantry)
			4	cups chicken broth
1	onion, chopped			Salt and freshly ground pepper to taste

1. Heat the olive oil in a large pot over medium heat.

2. Add the ground turkey, turkey sausage, smoked paprika, and Chile Molido. Cook for 6 to 8 minutes, stirring occasionally, or until the meat is done.

3. Add the onion, celery, bell peppers, and garlic and cook until the vegetables are soft.

4. Add the stewed tomatoes, chili mix, and chicken broth, stirring well.

5. Allow the chili to simmer, stirring occasionally.

6. Season with salt and pepper. Delicious served with grated cheese, chopped tomatoes, and corn chips.

Iris' Creamy Vegetable Chicken Noodle Soup

My beloved Iris, our house sister, rules the roost at my home in Chicago. I love her to pieces. Many times when someone in the family does not feel well, she makes this soup for us. All I can say is that this soup is wonderful when you don't feel so good—or when it's cold outside. When I taste it I think of all the love Iris gives to my family. She is a lady of many, many talents. Thank you, Iris, for the love and for this great soup recipe.

2	tablespoons olive oil
½	onion, diced
2	to 3 stalks celery, diced
2	cloves garlic, minced
2	quarts water
1	whole chicken, cut into boneless pieces
2	(15-ounce) cans mixed vegetables, drained
2	(10¾-ounce) cans cream of chicken soup
1	(10¾-ounce) can cream of mushroom soup
1	(15-ounce) can diced tomatoes, drained
1	teaspoon dried basil
¼	box (2 ounces) spaghetti, broken in half and cooked
2	tablespoons fresh parsley
	Salt and freshly ground black pepper to taste

1. Heat the olive oil in a medium stockpot over high heat.

2. Add the onion, celery, and garlic and cook for 6 to 8 minutes, or until the onion is translucent.

3. Add the water and the chicken pieces. Bring to a rolling boil for 5 minutes and then lower to a slow simmer for 20 minutes. Using a ladle, skim off any impurities that float to the top of the pot and discard.

4. Add the canned vegetables, cream soups, tomatoes, and dried basil.

5. Return the soup to a slow simmer.

6. Add the cooked pasta and chopped fresh parsley. Serve immediately or cool and freeze for later use.

Miso Broth with Soba Noodles and Tuna

MAKES 4 SERVINGS

This is an exceptional dish with beautiful Asian flavors and textures. On top of that, it is good for you. Soba noodles are chewy and fun to eat, and the tuna makes this a complete meal.

1	quart chicken or vegetable stock	1	cucumber, seeded and julienned
2	tablespoons miso paste	1	cup broccoli slaw (available in produce section)
1	(8-ounce) package soba noodles or vermicelli noodles, cooked and chilled	2	tablespoons dry roasted peanuts, crushed
2	tablespoons prepared sesame soy dressing	1	cup fresh bean sprouts
		¼	cup chopped fresh cilantro
4	(3 to 4 ounce) tuna fillets	1	serrano pepper, seeded and sliced
1	medium carrot, julienned		

1. Bring the stock to a boil in a saucepan and whisk in the miso paste until it has completely dissolved.

2. Place the cooked noodles in a large bowl and toss them with sesame soy dressing. Set aside.

3. Heat the tuna according to the recommended directions on the package.

4. Add the tuna, carrots, cucumbers, and broccoli slaw to the noodles. Pour in the hot stock. Stir well.

5. Garnish with the crushed peanuts, bean sprouts, cilantro, and serrano pepper. Serve warm.

Never lose an opportunity of seeing anything that is beautiful for beauty is God's handwriting—a wayside sacrament. Welcome it in every fair face, in every fair sky, in every fair flower, and thank God for it as a cup of blessing.
—RALPH WALDO EMERSON

IT IS ALWAYS NICE TO HAVE A LITTLE TASTE OF
something before you really start your meal, just to get your taste buds
going. Starters are especially fun to make when company is on its way.
My ceviche is terrific for a barbecue, and one of my all-time favorites
for anytime is tomato pie, for which I have Martha Stewart to thank.
She inspired the recipe and I took it one step further by adding my
own personal touches.

Probably the healthiest way to start a meal is with a great salad.
It can also be delicious—it doesn't have to be just healthy, you know.
Beets, although hated by some, are adored by others, including me.
When corn is in season and at its freshest, I also adore my corn salad.
Truthfully, a simple salad made of good, fresh greens and a simple
dressing is also hard to beat. And you don't get much healthier
than that.

Coleslaw

MAKES 8 TO 10 SERVINGS

This coleslaw was served at the first large-scale Common Threads event that we had in downtown Chicago. More than five hundred people showed up to support a wonderful cause and to enjoy foods from all over the world.

1	medium head cabbage (about 3 pounds), shredded or chopped	2	tablespoons stone-ground prepared mustard
2	large carrots, shredded	⅓	cup red wine vinegar
1	large onion, minced		Salt and freshly ground black pepper to taste
1	cup crème fraiche		

1. Mix the cabbage, carrots, and onion in a large bowl.

2. Whip the crème fraiche and the mustard in a separate bowl while slowly adding the vinegar.

3. Add the crème fraiche mixture to the cabbage and toss it all together.

4. Season with salt and pepper. Serve immediately or cover and chill before serving.

Fennel Coleslaw

MAKES 4 SERVINGS

This delicious slaw was created for the Common Threads World Festival by our friend, chef Jason Handelman of Fox & Obel Cafe. I love how it tastes on tacos and hope you will, too.

Vinaigrette

¾ cup apple cider vinegar

¼ cup lemon juice

½ cup vegetable oil

Sugar to taste

Salt and freshly ground black pepper to taste

Coleslaw

4 fennel bulbs, thinly sliced

1 head radicchio, cut in half, with core removed and sliced

½ red onion, thinly sliced

4 oranges, with sections cut in half

4 to 6 radishes, julienned

1. **For the vinaigrette,** pour the vinegar and lemon juice into a blender and blend on low speed.

2. Slowly stream in the oil and then add the sugar, salt, and pepper.

3. **For the coleslaw,** cover the sliced fennel with a damp paper towel to prevent any discoloration, or sprinkle with lemon juice. Prepare the remaining ingredients.

4. Combine the fennel, radicchio, onion, oranges, and radishes in a large bowl and gently mix with your hands. Add the vinaigrette to the coleslaw and toss again. The dish is ready to serve or can be chilled for later use.

Roasted Poblano Pepper Salad

MAKES 4 SERVINGS

This is a great way to put a little zip into your dinner.

5	to 6 poblano peppers	Olive oil to taste
1	white sweet (or red) onion, sliced	Salt and freshly ground black pepper to taste
2	tomatoes, seeded and sliced into thin wedges	Queso fresco or Farmer's cheese
	Fresh oregano to taste	

1. To roast the peppers, preheat the oven to 425 degrees. Coat the peppers with a little olive oil and place them on a half sheet pan and bake them for 10 to 15 minutes, turning them once. (Personally, I like to use sturdy tongs and hold the peppers over the open flame on a gas stove. If you try this method, be very careful not to drop the hot peppers.) Place the peppers in a bowl and cover with plastic wrap.

2. Remove the plastic from the bowl after 10 minutes and peel the skin off of the peppers. Take out the seeds and cut off the ends of the peppers. Lay the peppers out flat and slice them a little thicker than the onions.

3. In a bowl, combine the peppers, onion, tomatoes, oregano, oil, and salt and pepper. Toss to mix well.

4. Transfer to a serving dish, and crumble the queso fresco on top of the salad.

Fresh Asparagus Salad

This is a great salad to make in the spring when fresh asparagus is abundant. It is especially good with grilled foods. My mother used to feed me asparagus when I was a small child, and I have loved it ever since.

2	pounds asparagus, sliced on the bias	3	tablespoons extra virgin olive oil
1	shallot, minced	2	tablespoons sherry vinegar
2	cups shaved Parmesan cheese		Salt and freshly ground black pepper to taste

1. In a bowl, combine the asparagus, shallot, Parmesan cheese, olive oil, and vinegar. Season with salt and freshly ground pepper.

2. Cover and allow to marinate in the refrigerator for at least 2 hours. Bring to room temperature before serving.

Fresh Corn Salad

When sweet corn is in season this is a wonderfully simple salad that goes great with grilled meats and fish. I love to grill the ears on the fire to add a little char flavor to the salad.

8	ears corn, shucked	1	bell pepper, seeded and chopped
3	tablespoons extra virgin olive oil plus some for brushing the corn	1	jalapeño pepper, seeded and minced
6	fresh tomatoes, chopped	¼	cup chopped cilantro
2	cucumbers, peeled, seeded, and chopped		Salt and freshly ground black pepper to taste
2	green onions, minced	4	tablespoons white balsamic vinegar

1. Prepare the grill to medium high.

2. Brush the ears of corn with extra virgin olive oil.

3. Grill the corn until it is light brown, turning often for even cooking. When cool enough to handle, cut the corn off the ears.

4. Toss the corn with the tomatoes, cucumbers, greens onions, bell pepper, jalapeño, cilantro, salt and pepper, vinegar, and 3 tablespoons of the olive oil. Toss and marinate at least 2 hours in the refrigerator before serving. Bring to room temperature and serve with hamburgers or grilled fish.

Tomato Pie

This simple, savory pie has been a hit at many parties. People now request it all year long, but it's best when tomatoes are in season. It's fabulous with fried chicken.

Cheese Pastry

2½ cups self-rising flour, sifted

2 tablespoons unsalted butter, cold

2 tablespoons vegetable shortening, cold

¼ cup grated cheddar cheese or grated Pepper Jack cheese

½ cup buttermilk

Tomato Filling

2 tablespoons unsalted butter

½ Vidalia onion, chopped

1 stalk celery, chopped

2 cloves garlic, minced

1 jalapeño pepper, seeded and minced

3 cups baby pear tomatoes (red and yellow), cut in half lengthwise

2 tablespoons all-purpose flour

Salt and freshly ground black pepper to taste

1 egg white, beaten with 2 tablespoons water

2 tablespoons grated Parmesan cheese

1. **For the cheese pastry,** in a food processor, add the flour, butter, shortening, and grated cheese.

2. Using the pulse button on the food processor, process until coarse.

3. Gradually add the buttermilk—it will make a ball.

4. Remove from the food processor and refrigerate.

5. **For the tomato filling,** heat the butter in a sauté pan over medium heat. Add the onion, celery, garlic, and pepper. Cook until the vegetables are soft.

6. Add the tomatoes and the all-purpose flour, tossing well.

7. Season with salt and pepper, remove from the heat, and allow to cool.

8. **To assemble,** remove the dough from the refrigerator and split in half.

9. Coat an 8-inch tart or pie pan with vegetable spray.

10. On a lightly floured surface, roll the dough out in a circle, $^1/_4$-inch thick, and press into the pan. Avoid stretching the dough.

11. Fill with the tomato mixture.

12. Take the second ball and roll it into a flat disk, cutting it into strips with a sharp knife or pastry wheel. Place the strips over the top of the pie. Then lay the strips in the opposite direction, creating a basket-weave design.

13. Refrigerate the pie and preheat the oven to 400 degrees.

14. Remove the pie from the refrigerator, and brush with the egg-white wash, sprinkle with Parmesan cheese and place in the oven. Bake for 10 minutes.

15. Reduce the heat to 375 degrees and bake the pie for 35 minutes. Cover with foil if the pie edges begin to brown too quickly. Bake the pie until it begins to bubble. Serve warm or at room temperature.

Anne Bloomstrand's Hash Brown Potato Salad

MAKES 4 SERVINGS

When I cook Anne's wonderful recipes they take me back to those amazing meals she created for us in Chicago, the place that became my home because she always made it taste like home.

3	pounds new potatoes, diced	2	cups (1 pint) cherry tomatoes, cut in half
4	tablespoons corn oil	1	red onion, diced
½	pound bacon	⅔	cup mayonnaise
2	tablespoons mustard seeds	4	tablespoons chopped fresh parsley
6	tablespoons apple cider vinegar		
½	teaspoon chopped fresh rosemary		

1. Preheat the oven to 400 degrees.

2. Steam the diced potatoes over boiling water for 6 to 8 minutes.

3. Toss the potatoes in a large bowl with the corn oil. Place the potatoes in a single layer on a half sheet pan and bake until they are crispy, turning often.

4. Meanwhile, fry the bacon and drain. When cool enough to handle, crumble the bacon and set aside.

5. Drain all but 1 tablespoon of grease from the skillet and add the mustard seeds. Cover and cook for 3 to 4 minutes or until you hear a popping sound from the seeds.

6. Add 4 tablespoons of vinegar to the seeds, cover, and heat for 1 to 2 minutes. Add to the potatoes and continue to bake for another 5 minutes.

7. In a large bowl, toss the remaining 2 tablespoons of vinegar, the rosemary, tomatoes, onion, mayonnaise, and parsley.

8. Add the potatoes and all but 2 tablespoons of crumbled bacon.

9. Toss and garnish with the remaining bacon and the additional chopped parsley, if desired.

Mixed Roasted Beets with Sliced Fennel Salad

MAKES 8 SERVINGS

This is a simple yet elegant salad packed with very distinct flavors that work extremely well together.

3   baby beets, trimmed

3   red beets, trimmed

3   golden beets, trimmed

Extra virgin olive oil to taste

Salt and freshly ground black pepper to taste

3   tablespoons champagne vinegar

5   tablespoons white balsamic vinegar

1   fennel bulb, thinly sliced (keep in water with a little lemon juice)

1. Preheat the oven to 325 degrees.

2. Combine the beets in a bowl. Drizzle olive oil over them and toss. Place them on a sheet pan and sprinkle with salt and pepper. Roasting the beets may take up to 2 hours depending on the size. Smaller beets will take 45 minutes to 1 hour to cook.

3. When the baby beets are done, place them in a bowl and cover them with plastic. Return the large beets to the oven and finish cooking. Transfer to a bowl and cover with plastic. Allow to cool 10 minutes.

4. When they are cooled, the skin should just peel off. If not, use a paring knife to remove the thin outer skin. Thinly slice the beets, return them to the bowl, and add the vinegars. Marinate the beets for at least 30 minutes.

5. Overlap the beets on a plate, then drizzle with more olive oil and season with more salt and pepper.

6. Add the fennel and serve.

NOTE: To keep the color from bleeding, store the red beets in a separate bowl until it is time to serve them.

Jicama and Arugula Salad with Lime-Cilantro Dressing

MAKES 4 SERVINGS

Strong flavors that complement each other perfectly plus many different textures make this salad just right for almost any occasion.

1	fresh jicama, julienned	1	cup chopped fresh cilantro
6	to 8 ounces fresh arugula		Salt and freshly ground black pepper to taste
		½	tablespoon Dijon mustard
Dressing		¼	cup olive oil
⅛	teaspoon ground cumin		
¾	cup lime juice		

1. **For the dressing,** warm a sauté pan over medium heat, then toast the cumin until the aroma begins to release and set aside.

2. Mix the lime juice, cilantro, salt, pepper, and mustard in a standard blender or with a small emersion blender.

3. Pour in a steady stream of olive oil while blending. Add the toasted cumin.

4. When the dressing is finished, taste it for balance and adjust seasonings if necessary.

5. **To assemble the salad,** toss the sliced jicama with 2 tablespoons dressing.

6. Arrange the arugula in a chilled serving bowl. Top with the jicama and just before serving, toss with the remaining dressing.

Classic Ceviche

Even though there is no cooking involved, the acid in the citrus juice actually "cooks" the fish. I use a red onion in this because it has great color and adds so much more life to the dish than a regular Spanish or white onion.

1 pound mahi-mahi, cut in medium cubes (or your choice of fish, such as white bass, halibut, tilapia, or snapper)

1½ to 2 cups fresh lime or lemon juice

Salt to taste

½ teaspoon sugar

1 red onion, diced

1 serrano pepper, seeded and diced

1 avocado, diced

Freshly ground black pepper to taste

Olive oil

1. Place the fish in a glass container. Combine the lime juice, salt, and sugar and pour over the fish. Cover and refrigerate 4 to 6 hours, then drain gently to keep the shape of the fish.

2. Meanwhile in a separate bowl, mix the other ingredients, leaving the avocados for last. Chop the avocados just before serving in order to keep that wonderful green color.

3. Mix gently with the fish. Taste the ceviche to determine if the flavors are working together. Try to balance the sweet with the salty and the sour with the spicy. Adjust the seasoning accordingly and serve.

Shrimp Cocktail

Ideally this classic appetizer starts with quality shrimp and ends with a sauce that is so delicious it makes you wonder if the shrimp is just a way for you to get the sauce into your mouth after all.

1	pound cooked large or jumbo shrimp, shelled and deveined	½	red onion, diced
1	cup ketchup	2	avocados, coarsely chopped
1	cup cocktail sauce	⅓	cup fresh lime juice
1	cup orange soda or ½ cup orange juice		Hot sauce
1	cup roughly chopped cilantro		Salt and freshly ground black pepper to taste

1. Rinse the shrimp, drain, and set aside in the refrigerator until ready to serve.

2. Combine the ketchup, cocktail sauce, orange soda, cilantro, onion, avocados, lime juice, hot sauce, and salt and pepper in a large, nonreactive bowl.

3. Cover and chill in the refrigerator for at least 1 hour before serving.

4. Adjust the seasoning, adding more hot sauce, salt, or pepper to taste. Serve with the cooked and chilled shrimp.

Goat Cheese Roll

MAKES 8 TO 10 SERVINGS

What's a little cheese spread? In the South, I think we invented cheese balls. Well, this one's more fancy and really great served before dinner with crackers.

8 ounces goat cheese, softened	½ teaspoon freshly ground black pepper
½ cup coarsely chopped toasted pecans	½ teaspoon paprika
	Pinch of salt

1. Roll the goat cheese into a log. Combine the pecans, ground pepper, paprika, and salt on a baking sheet or a wide bowl. Roll the goat cheese log in the seasoned nuts and refrigerate for at least I hour. Serve with crackers.

Heirloom Tomatoes with Buffalo Mozzarella and Fresh Basil

MAKES 6 TO 8 SERVINGS

This salad must be made in late summer when the tomatoes are perfect. I love that heirloom tomatoes are available everywhere now, but if you have a little plot of land or even a few big pots, I would suggest you grow your own because they are so worth it. Nothing tastes better than a ripe heirloom tomato off the vine—one that has never been refrigerated—served with mozzarella and fresh basil. I like to drizzle mine with a little extra virgin olive oil. This dish is perfectly lovely, and so great tasting!

6	to 8 assorted heirloom tomatoes, sliced	1	tablespoon roughly chopped fresh rosemary
3	balls fresh buffalo mozzarella cheese, sliced	1	tablespoon roughly chopped fresh thyme
1	bunch fresh basil leaves	1	tablespoon roughly chopped fresh parsley
¼	cup extra virgin olive oil		
½	cup balsamic vinegar	1	tablespoon roughly chopped fresh oregano
	Salt and freshly ground black pepper to taste		

1. Arrange the tomato slices in one layer on a large dish. Place a mozzarella slice and fresh basil leaf on top of each tomato.

2. Right before serving, drizzle the olive oil and balsamic vinegar over the tomato stacks. Sprinkle with salt and pepper.

3. Sprinkle the freshly chopped herbs over the plate to finish.

Mache and Baby Spinach Salad with Fuji Apples, Toasted Pecans, and Parmesan Shavings

MAKES 6 TO 8 SERVINGS

Mache is one of the most delicious and tender greens. Now you can often find it at your supermarket. Fuji apples are great with this recipe. Add toasted pecans with some good Parmesan, and you have a perfectly fabulous salad.

Vinaigrette

½ cup balsamic vinegar

1 teaspoon grainy prepared mustard

1 clove garlic, minced

1 teaspoon salt

¼ teaspoon black pepper

1½ cups olive oil

Salad

4 to 6 ounces mache

4 ounces fresh spinach leaves

1 Fuji apple (or whatever is in season), thinly sliced

1 teaspoon fresh parsley

Toasted pecan halves

2 to 4 ounces shredded Parmesan cheese

Salt and pepper to taste

1. **For the vinaigrette,** combine the vinegar, mustard, garlic, salt, and pepper in a small bowl.

2. While whisking slowly, add the oil. Mix well.

3. **For the salad,** clean the greens under cold water and pat them dry, then place a damp paper towel over them to prevent wilting.

4. Place the greens in a serving bowl.

5. Toss the sliced apples in the vinaigrette and arrange on the greens.

6. Add the parsley and, using a peeler, shave a wedge of Parmesan cheese over the top.

7. Season with salt and pepper to taste. Before serving, toss the salad with the remaining vinaigrette.

Arugula Salad with Toasted Salted Walnuts and Asian Pears

MAKES 6 TO 8 SERVINGS

Arugula is my favorite of all greens, probably because I grew up on greens that were slightly bitter. Arugula, which can easily be grown in your kitchen garden, is best when it is picked young. We enjoy it frequently at Ms. Winfrey's estate in Montecito. There is not a better salad than one made with arugula, walnuts, and pears. To make it even more wonderful, add some Gorgonzola cheese.

Pear Vinaigrette

½	cup white balsamic vinegar
1	clove garlic, minced
1	teaspoon sugar
1½	cups olive oil
½	pear, peeled and diced (small)
1	tablespoon chopped fresh parsley
	Salt and freshly ground black pepper to taste

Salad

1	cup whole walnuts
	Olive oil
	Salt to taste
4	(6-ounce) bags fresh arugula
1	pear, thinly sliced
1	(4-ounce) roll plain goat cheese, crumbled

1. **For the vinaigrette,** combine the vinegar, garlic, and sugar.

2. Add the oil slowly, whisk, and then add the diced pears.

3. Add the chopped parsley and mix well.

4. Season with salt and pepper and set aside.

5. **For the salad,** preheat the oven to 300 degrees.

6. In a small bowl, toss the walnuts with a little bit of oil and salt, and then place them in a single layer on a sheet pan. Place in the oven and toast for 5 to 10 minutes. Remove and cool.

7. Wash and pat dry the arugula. Place a damp paper towel over it to prevent wilting.

8. When ready to serve, toss the arugula with the vinaigrette. Top with the walnuts, sliced pear, and crumbled goat cheese. Serve on chilled salad plates.

Addie Mae's Potato Salad

MAKES 6 TO 8 SERVINGS

This is my mother's prized potato salad. You will love it.

2	pounds Yukon gold or new red potatoes, peeled and cubed	1	teaspoon celery seeds or 4 celery ribs, finely chopped
½	cup sweet pickle relish		Salt and freshly ground black pepper to taste
5	hard-boiled eggs, chopped		
2	teaspoons yellow prepared mustard	4	slices bacon, cooked and crumbled for garnish
1	cup mayonnaise	1	red bell pepper, chopped, for garnish
½	onion, chopped		Cider vinegar to taste

1. Cover the potatoes with water and cook in a large pot over medium-high heat until just tender, about 6 minutes. Check the potatoes frequently, making sure they do not overcook.

2. Drain the potatoes in a colander and run cold water over them to let them cool. Transfer the potatoes back to the pot.

3. Add the relish, eggs, mustard, mayonnaise, onion, celery seeds, and salt and pepper, mixing gently. (For variety, I sometimes use dill relish instead of the sweet relish.)

4. Garnish with bacon, red pepper, and a sprinkling of vinegar, if desired.

*What lies behind us and what lies before us are
tiny matters compared to what lies within us.*
—Ralph Waldo Emerson

SINCE THE CREATION OF BREAD PEOPLE HAVE
searched for the perfect ingredients to complement it, making the
perfect, quick and healthy meal. The key is good-quality multigrain
bread, and healthy ingredients. I grew up on egg salad sandwiches, and
our pimento cheese makes the ideal tea party or wedding sandwich—
something I was very familiar with growing up in the South.

Ham Panini

MAKES 2 TO 3 SANDWICHES

There's a reason why just about every culture in the Western world has a version of the ham and cheese sandwich—they're delicious! I hope you love my version as much as I do.

4 to 6 slices whole grain bread
Cherry mustard for spreading
Mayonnaise for spreading

½ pound baked ham, thinly sliced

¼ pound provolone cheese, thinly sliced

2 to 3 ounces fresh mache greens
Olive oil for drizzling or butter for spreading

1. Preheat the oven to 375 degrees.

2. Preheat a sauté pan over medium heat. Take 2 slices of bread and spread cherry mustard on one piece and mayonnaise on the other.

3. Place about 3 ounces of ham on one piece of bread.

4. On top of the ham, lay 1 or 2 slices of cheese and 4 leaves of mache.

5. Spread the butter or drizzle the olive oil onto the outsides of the bread.

6. Place the sandwich in the pan and brown for about 1 minute per side, then place the sandwich in the oven on a baking sheet for 3 or 4 minutes, or until the cheese melts.

7. Remove from the oven. Slice and serve.

Turkey Panini

We should eat turkey and cranberry more than once a year, and we shouldn't have to fall asleep afterward. This healthy sandwich will keep you on your toes.

4   to 6 slices whole wheat bread
     Cranberry horseradish for spreading
     Mayonnaise for spreading

½   pound grilled turkey, thinly sliced

¼   pound Swiss cheese, thinly sliced

3   to 4 ounces fresh baby spinach
     Freshly ground black pepper to taste
     Butter or olive oil for spreading

1. Preheat the oven to 375 degrees.

2. Place a sauté pan over medium-low heat. Spread cranberry horseradish on half of the bread and mayonnaise on the other half.

3. Place about 3 ounces of grilled turkey on the bread slices with horseradish.

4. Lay Swiss cheese and baby spinach on top of the turkey, and grind some black pepper over the top. Place the mayonnaise-coated bread slices on top to make sandwiches.

5. Spread butter or drizzle olive oil onto the outsides of the bread.

6. Place the sandwich in the pan and brown for about 1 minute per side, then place each sandwich on a baking sheet and bake in the oven for 3 to 4 minutes, or until the cheese melts.

7. Remove from the oven. Slice and serve.

Prosciutto and Focaccia Sandwich

Focaccia is so good it's sometimes eaten on its own. Add some ham and other goodies to it, and it's almost too good.

Focaccia

Olive tapenade for spreading

2   plum tomatoes, sliced

Extra virgin olive oil for drizzling

½   pound prosciutto de Parma, thinly sliced

Fresh mozzarella, thinly sliced

Fresh basil leaves

Freshly ground black pepper

1. Preheat the oven to 375 degrees.

2. Split the focaccia in half to make two slices.

3. On one side of the bread, spread the olive tapenade and lay 3 to 4 tomato slices on top.

4. On the other half, drizzle some olive oil and lay 5 to 6 slices of the prosciutto on top.

5. Add 4 slices of fresh mozzarella and 4 to 5 fresh basil leaves.

6. Add freshly ground black pepper and close the sandwich.

7. Place in the oven for 3 to 4 minutes or until the cheese begins to melt.

8. Cut into 2 or 3 individual sandwiches and serve warm.

Addie Mae's Hamburger

MAKES 4 HAMBURGERS

Growing up in Florida my favorite time of the year was summer. Even though it was scorching hot, my mother would make these amazing hamburgers. They are very simple. I think it was the cast-iron skillet she cooked them in that made them special. I love the juicy burgers, served with sun-ripened tomatoes and crispy lettuce. The other best part is the Roman Meal hamburger bun. This is a great combination.

1½ pounds ground chuck

Salt and freshly ground black pepper to taste

Toppings

4 Multigrain hamburger buns, toasted

4 slices American cheese, or blue cheese

8 slices ripe tomato

4 slices Vidalia onion

4 pieces crispy iceberg lettuce

Mayonnaise (optional)

Mustard (optional)

Ketchup (optional)

1. Place a heavy cast-iron skillet over medium heat.

2. Season the meat with salt and pepper. Shape into 4 (6-ounce) hamburger patties. Place in the skillet and cook until completely done and no red remains in the center.

3. Assemble the burgers on toasted Roman Meal buns with 1 slice of cheese, 2 slices of tomatoes, 1 slice of sweet onion, 1 piece of iceberg lettuce, and mayonnaise, mustard, and ketchup if desired.

CHAPTER 7

Supper—Time to Nourish and Reflect

J ust the sound of the word *supper* gives me pleasure. It is that beautiful time in the evening when we begin to wind down and get comfortable with the ones we love. We sit, we sigh, and we share our stories along with the last meal of the day. Supper is a time for goodness and warmth, for one-dish wonders paired with a simple salad and maybe a bite of dessert for a treat.

As the day is closing, cook your loved ones and yourself a nice meal. Turn off the television and share some good conversation. Life is hard, and we depend on those close to us to lift us up and rejuvenate us. A few simple words can make a world of difference to a person's emotional growth. When you arrive at the doorstep of your home in the evening, leave out the bad and bring in the good. Step inside, put on some nice music, and let the healing begin!

I love soft music when I am cooking. Sometimes I like to play music that matches the theme of my cooking. I swear I make a better paella when I am listening to Spanish guitar music. And there's nothing like cranking up the blues for a down-home jambalaya cooking session. Music makes the food taste better when you sit down, too, because it puts you in the right mood. People always talk about being in the mood for love, but what about being in the mood to cook? Music can do that for you—and a pleasant cooking space helps, too.

I am fortunate to have a wonderful kitchen in which to work—at last! It is spacious and clean in design, and it allows me to cook large meals for heaps of friends and family—and for my charity, Common Threads. I am constantly amazed at how much people are willing to pay for an Art Smith meal. I know my food is good, but I also think it has something to do with my employer. She is loved by so many people. I can just hear the comments now:"I can't wait to eat what Oprah eats!"

My beloved Oprah adores home-cooked, healthful meals. This does not surprise me because in my years of cooking I have found that the busier people are, the simpler they like their food. Something can be simple and of the highest quality at the same time. It's all about finding and using the best ingredients available.

Many people get nervous when they have me over for a meal. This, I do not understand. I like very simple foods. And I love a meal prepared by friends. Who does not love a meal he or she did not have to prepare? Sometimes I like their food better than my own.

Through the years I have been lucky enough to eat in the finest restaurants in America. I have eaten every possible precious food ever created by famous and fashionable chefs. Even so, I still enjoy a great baked potato with all the trimmings. To go with it, I love a nice perfectly cooked steak, served with a little mustard sauce. That is a wonderful supper to me. Simple, delicious. And not a tower of tiny ingredients or a cloud of foam anywhere in sight! Just real food, prepared well, and maybe with a little bluegrass music playing in the background for inspiration.

Beef, Chicken, and Pork

We live in a country that takes prides in its high quality beef. For more than forty years my family has raised some of the finest Angus beef in America. My parents unfortunately have befriended most of the herd so it has been a while since they have sold any cows. Be careful about making friends with your food! The first time I heard how wonderful Kobe beef is I thought, *If someone massaged me and fed me beer, I would be less tense, too!*

On the other side of the fence, chickens are not the friendliest creatures in the world, but that doesn't mean I want to run out to a farm and ring one's neck. I'll leave that to the farmers and butchers. One thing I know is that I could not live without a nice

roasted chicken every now and then for supper. Brine the chicken, roast it in a pan, and it will come out perfect. Always make a raft of vegetables to set the bird on, and all of that flavor will go right into your chicken. This works great with pork roasts, too.

I've made some really wonderful pork roasts recently in my wood-burning brick oven, but your trusty kitchen oven can do the same job as a fancy brick oven. Just make sure it is calibrated properly, and that it has a thermometer inside.

Roasting meats and vegetables in the oven makes for a wonderful, easy supper. I do it all the time, and everyone loves it. When they see me relaxing before a meal, sometimes folks get scared that in my old age I have forgotten to start cooking, but eventually a great aroma begins wafting through the house and all questions are put to rest.

Pizza, Sides, and Desserts

Another great one-dish wonder I love is tuna casserole, made with really great packaged tuna, good pasta, fresh vegetables, and a nice béchamel sauce. Sprinkle some quality Italian Parmesan on this lovely dish and bake it until it is bubbly. My goodness, that is a dish that will have you believing you are sitting in the best, most charming rustic restaurant in all of the Italian countryside!

Want to get your kids to eat their vegetables and still enjoy what they are eating? My mother's broccoli casserole never fails. Sadly, the casserole has gotten a bad rap. It all goes back to ingredients, and the unfounded notion that "simple food" equals "inferior ingredients." If I knew I could convince America that simple foods made with quality ingredients could change their lives, I would set out on the road with a large stock pot to stand on, and just preach! But I don't think that would be a good use of my time, so let me just tell you right now: if you use quality ingredients along with time-saving simple recipes, these dishes will set you free!

Making the Family Happy

In my "Ask Art" column on Oprah.com, I often answer questions from mothers across the country asking for advice on how to satisfy everyone at the supper table. My feeling is that if the whole family were involved in preparing a meal, there would be a better chance that everyone would start to like the same things. Many adults—and almost every kid I have met—like being involved in the creation of their meals. How many children refuse to eat a dish until they know exactly what is in it? Note: Kids love texture, so if you want to score points with them, give them something with a little crunch—anything they can sink their teeth into.

We often focus on how to get kids to eat better, but what about ourselves, the adults? Thank God science has proven that a little dark chocolate is actually good for you. Unfortunately, I have eaten my lifetime medicinal allotment already. People keep sending chocolate to me, nonetheless. The word is out and you know I love it, but if I ate every piece of chocolate that arrived in my mailbox somebody would break a bottle of champagne over my head and christen me the SS *Art*. It does have a nice ring to it, but I really don't want to go there!

It's not just chocolate with me. I simply love to eat and trust me, I never miss a meal. I love to dine, too, which is so far beyond merely eating. I love the smells, the tastes, the rituals, the conversation, and the company. And suppertime is the best opportunity to let down your guard and relax. It is a meal we should never miss, if for no other reason than to simply come together at the end of the day and say a few nice things to each other after the world has beaten us down and we have run ourselves ragged. People can be so mean, but may God bless them and allow us to go forward.

Simple Formula, High Quality

I have put together some simple supper recipes for you that I know will be easy to prepare. Your job is to go out and shop for the freshest ingredients to make these dishes the best they can be. Of course, as with any meal, make sure there is love in your heart when you are cooking, because food without love just does not taste good, no matter who has cooked it. On a practical note, I know that when we are cooking we all like to taste and taste and taste some more, but what happens is we burn out on the flavors and we lose our ability to be a good judge of how the dish is coming along. It's especially important with these one-dish wonders not to over-taste while you're cooking. My suggestion is to taste the dish in the beginning and at the very end.

With supper, keep the formula simple and the quality high. Keep the dishes uncomplicated, and the conversation elaborate. No one ever complains about being told how much they are loved in new and creative ways. Most of all, focus on the people you are with at the close of yet another day.

Enjoy your supper!

MY DEAR FRIEND TODD HATOFF OF ALLEN

Brothers, one of Chicago's oldest meat producers, has taught me so much about fine meats. Because there is such a huge range of quality available, you should always have a great meat purveyor in your life. Shop in a supermarket that still employs a hands-on, knowledgeable butcher—not just some kid re-stocking shelves in a white coat. You should feel the same way about fishmongers. Only shop at a supermarket for fish if they have someone who is in charge and responsible for obtaining the freshest fish available, caring for it properly, and knowing when to pitch it when it has not sold quickly enough. My advice to you is to never sell yourself short in the meat and fish category. Find someone you trust, and become a repeat customer.

Pistachio-Crusted Chicken with Coconut-Chili-Ginger Sauce

MAKES 6 TO 8 SERVINGS

This dish, which I created for a special guest of Ms. Winfrey, is one of my most frequently requested new dishes. Everyone asks for seconds. We have served it over and over again to our guests. If you love the flavors of Asia, this is right up your pad Thai alley. My sous chef, Rey Villalobos, crusts his chicken ahead of time and refrigerates it, which he says makes the crust stay on better. The sauce is my most famous. I've even had people tell me they could drink this sauce. It can be made ahead of time because it keeps well in the refrigerator.

Coconut-Chili-Ginger Sauce

1	tablespoon unsalted butter
2	shallots, minced
2	blades lemongrass, chopped
3	(½-inch) pieces fresh ginger, thinly sliced
1	cup sweet white wine
2	cups chicken broth
2	tablespoons Thai red curry paste
2	tablespoons Chinese black bean chili sauce
1	(8-ounce) can coconut milk
½	cup (1 stick) unsalted butter, softened and cut into pieces
	Salt and freshly ground black pepper to taste

Pistachio-Crusted Chicken

4	brined, boneless chicken breasts (see recipe on page 237)
1	quart buttermilk
1	pound salted pistachios, shelled and toasted
1	cup grated Parmesan cheese
¼	cup fresh thyme
¼	cup chopped fresh rosemary
¼	cup chopped fresh parsley
2	cups all-purpose flour
	Salt and freshly ground black pepper to taste
	Grapeseed oil to taste

1. **For the sauce,** in a medium saucepan over medium-high heat, add the tablespoon of butter, the shallots, lemongrass, ginger slices, and wine. Reduce to half.

2. Add the broth, red curry paste, and Chinese black bean chili sauce and reduce to half again.

3. Add the coconut milk and reduce to half a third time.

4. Remove from the heat and whisk the bits of butter into the sauce until all the butter has been incorporated. Season with salt and pepper.

5. If you reheat, do not allow the sauce to boil, or the butter will separate.

6. **For the chicken,** remove the chicken from the brine and cut in half. With a meat mallet, pound until $1/4$-inch thick and place in a nonreactive bowl. Pour the buttermilk over the chicken, cover, and let sit for at least 1 hour in the refrigerator.

7. In a food processor, place half of the pistachios, half of the Parmesan cheese, and half of the herbs. Pulse 5 or 6 times until the mixture is finely chopped. Transfer to a bowl. Repeat this step with the rest of the pistachios and combine with the other pistachio mixture.

8. Preheat the oven to 250 degrees.

9. Place the flour in another bowl and season it with salt and pepper.

10. Remove the chicken from the refrigerator and prepare it for assembly.

11. Preheat a large nonstick sauté pan over medium-low heat with a thin coating of grapeseed oil.

12. Remove one breast, shake off any excess buttermilk, and dust the breast with flour on each side.

13. Dip only one side of the chicken back in the buttermilk and press pistachios onto that side. Repeat that step with all of the chicken.

14. Place the chicken in the sauté pan, pistachio side down, and cook for 2 to 3 minutes. Turn and cook the other side for 2 to 3 minutes.

15. Place in the oven to finish cooking for 8 to 10 minutes. Remove, let rest for 5 minutes, and then slice to serve with the Coconut-Chile-Ginger Sauce.

Chicken Mole

One of my favorite dishes comes from Oaxaca, Mexico, where chocolate is used to flavor the wonderfully spicy sauce. My sous chef, Rey Villalobos, often makes this beautiful dish for our guests.

Chicken

1   whole chicken, cut into 8 pieces

1   whole onion, peeled

2   quarts cold water

2   tablespoons olive oil

Mole Sauce

1/2   cup canola oil

2   slices white bread

2   10-inch corn tortillas

1/2   pound ancho chiles (soaked in hot water, seeded and stemmed)

1   tablespoon creamy peanut butter

1/4   cup raisins

1/2   square Mexican chocolate

1/2   tablespoon toasted sesame seeds

1. In a large stockpot combine the chicken, onion, water, and oil. Bring to a boil for 5 minutes and then reduce the heat and simmer for 15 minutes.

2. Remove the chicken from the stock and set stock aside.

3. **For the sauce,** in a frying pan over medium-high heat, add the canola oil and fry each side of the bread until golden brown. Use the same technique for the tortillas and set aside to cool.

4. Place the ancho chiles, peanut butter, raisins, chocolate, sesame seeds, and 1 cup of the reserved stock in a blender and blend. The consistency of the sauce will be thick. Strain the sauce.

5. In a large pot, add 2 tablespoons olive oil over medium-low heat, slowly add the strained thickened mole sauce, and fry.

6. Thin out the sauce with the extra stock while whisking. The sauce is ready when it coats a spoon.

7. **To assemble the dish,** add the chicken to the sauce and coat. Adjust the salt and serve. Freeze any leftover stock for later use.

Cheese Enchiladas

Enchiladas are a great buffet main course for people of any age. This is an authentic recipe. You can find the chiles at a Mexican market, and don't forget the traditional enchilada cheese to give it the right texture.

Sauce

½ pound ancho chiles, seeded, stemmed, and soaked in hot water until tender

¼ pound guajillo chiles, seeded, stemmed, and soaked in hot water until tender

1 clove garlic

1 pinch of cumin

Salt to taste

½ cup chicken stock

Stuffing

1 pound mild cheddar or Monterey Jack cheese, grated

1 onion, diced

1 cup peanut oil

12 (8- or 10-inch) corn tortillas

Garnishes

½ head of lettuce, shredded

2 medium tomatoes, diced

1 medium onion, sliced

3 avocadoes, sliced

Sour cream

1. **For the sauce,** in a blender combine the chiles, garlic, cumin, salt, and chicken stock and blend until smooth. Test for saltiness. Pour the sauce into a large shallow bowl and set it aside.

2. Preheat the oven to 350 degrees.

3. **For the stuffing,** blend the grated cheese and onion together in a bowl.

4. **To assemble,** in a frying pan, heat the peanut oil over medium-high heat. Dip a tortilla quickly (about 10 seconds) into the hot oil and remove. Dip the same tortilla quickly into the sauce and place on a plate.

5. When you have done 3 tortillas, place the stuffing in the tortillas and roll gently.

6. Place the rolled enchiladas into a lightly greased 13 x 9-inch baking dish. Transfer to the oven and bake for 10 minutes.

7. Place each garnish ingredient in its own bowl, and set the bowls on the table for guests to garnish as they desire.

Split Roasted Herbed Chicken

Roasted chicken is one dish people never get tired of eating. I love serving it at a nice, casual supper with friends.

2	whole chickens (skin on, spine removed)	¼	cup chopped fresh parsley or cilantro
4	large cloves garlic, minced	1	teaspoon dried sage
1	cup (2 sticks) unsalted butter, cut into 16 pieces and softened	1	teaspoon red pepper flakes
¼	cup chopped fresh rosemary		Salt and freshly ground black pepper to taste
¼	cup chopped fresh thyme		

1. Preheat the oven to 350 degrees.

2. Lay the chickens flat on an oiled half sheet pan or baking sheet.

3. In a large bowl, combine the garlic, butter, rosemary, thyme, parsley, sage, and red pepper flakes. Stir to mix well.

4. Gently lift the skin and rub with the compounded herb butter underneath the skin. Be careful not to tear the skin. Rub any excess butter on the other sides of the chicken.

5. Add salt and pepper and place the chickens in the oven for 30 to 45 minutes, or until the chicken internal temperature reaches 160 degrees and juices run clear.

NOTE: For a crispy skin, hold chicken under the broiler quickly, and then serve.

Grilled Turkey Breast

I brine all of my large pieces of meat or poultry, not only for the flavor, but also for the tenderness. You should try one whole day (twenty-four hours) of brining, and see if you don't notice a difference between that meat and unbrined meat, especially larger pieces.

1 (2-pound) turkey breast, bone-in and brined (see recipe on page 236)

Rub

10 to 12 cloves garlic, minced

½ cup chopped fresh rosemary

½ cup chopped fresh thyme

½ cup chopped fresh parsley

¼ cup chopped fresh oregano

¼ cup chopped fresh sage

½ cup paprika

1 teaspoon cayenne pepper

1½ cups olive oil

Salt freshly ground black pepper to taste

1. Preheat the grill and oil the grates. If using charcoal, designate high heat and low heat spots in order to control how quickly the food cooks, as some larger pieces of meat require more time.

2. Remove the turkey from the brine and discard the brining liquid.

3. **Make the rub** by combining the garlic, rosemary, thyme, parsley, oregano, sage, paprika, cayenne, and olive oil in a large mixing bowl.

4. Rub the mixture all over the turkey, place it on a half sheet pan, and sprinkle with salt and pepper.

5. When the coals are hot, place the turkey skin side down and sear that side first. This will take 2 to 4 minutes. Try not to move the turkey around during this step.

6. Flip the turkey to the other side and repeat the searing process.

7. Move the turkey to where the heat is not as intense and cover the grill.

8. Check every 10 to 15 minutes using a meat thermometer or instant-read

thermometer. The turkey is done when the internal temperature reaches 160 to 165 degrees.

9. Remove the turkey and let it rest for 6 minutes. Carve and serve.

Shank Ham with Addie Mae's Fig Jam

MAKES 8 SERVINGS

My mother has a great big fig tree that looks as if it could touch the sky. She always saves a few figs for me, and a few for her beloved birds. What a great way to share food! Rey came up with the idea of glazing shank ham with this wonderful jam, and it turned out to be a perfect match. If you have the time and the figs, make my mother's jam. If not, you can find good fig jam at the store.

Glaze

1	jar of Addie Mae's Fig Jam recipe (see recipe on page 165) or 1 cup fig jam
1	cup pineapple juice
½	cup brown sugar
2	tablespoons molasses
¼	cup maple syrup
½	tablespoon grainy prepared mustard
¼	teaspoon ground nutmeg
½	teaspoon ground cinnamon
2	tablespoons butter

Ham

1	(5-pound) shank ham, bone-in and spiral cut if possible
10	to 15 whole cloves
	Brown sugar

1. Preheat the oven to 350 degrees.

2. **For the glaze,** in a medium saucepan over medium heat, combine the fig jam, pineapple juice, sugar, molasses, maple syrup, mustard, nutmeg, and cinnamon. Bring to a low simmer for 5 minutes, stirring until all the sugar has dissolved. Whisk in the butter, remove from the heat, and set aside.

3. **For the ham,** place it in a roasting pan and make slits across the ham about 1½ inches apart.

4. Insert the cloves as desired.

5. Ladle the glaze over the ham and pat with brown sugar.

6. Cover the ham with foil and place it in the oven. Every 20 minutes baste the ham with the drippings.

7. After 1 hour 20 minutes, check the temperature with an instant-read thermometer. When it hits 160 degrees, remove from the oven and set aside to rest. After 10 minutes, carve and serve.

Addie Mae's Fig Jam

MAKES 7 QUARTS

This is my mother's famous fig jam. It obviously goes well with ham, but it also turns a piece of toast into a meal.

6	quarts boiling water	1	quart water
6	quarts fresh figs	7	slices lemon
5	to 6 cups sugar	7	sticks cinnamon

1. Pour boiling water over the figs and let them stand 15 to 20 minutes.

2. Drain and thoroughly rinse the figs in cold water.

3. Pat the figs dry and remove the stems.

4. Crush and measure the amount of figs before placing them in a Dutch oven.

5. Add $1/2$ cup of sugar for each cup of crushed figs.

6. Add the water and bring to a rapid boil over high heat. Reduce the heat and simmer uncovered, for $1 1/2$ to 2 hours, or until thick. Stir occasionally to prevent sticking.

7. Ladle the jam into hot sterilized jars, leaving $1/4$ inch of headspace.

8. Add 1 lemon slice and 1 stick of cinnamon to each jar. Remove any air bubbles.

9. Wipe the rims and adjust the lids. Process in a boiling water bath for 10 minutes.

10. Carefully remove the jars from the water with a jar lifter or sturdy tongs. Place on a kitchen towel or wire rack to cool for 12 to 24 hours. Jar lids will make a popping sound as they cool. Store any jars that don't seal in the refrigerator for 2 to 3 weeks.

Butterfly Pork Loin with Garlic, Red Pepper Flakes, and Cider Vinegar

MAKES 6 SERVINGS

In this recipe we butterfly a pork loin and cook it with garlic, red pepper, and cider vinegar. The rosemary gives it a wonderful Tuscan flavor.

Rub

1	small onion, diced
10	cloves garlic, crushed or minced
½	cup chopped fresh thyme
¼	cup chopped fresh rosemary
½	cup extra virgin olive oil
2	tablespoons red pepper flakes

Freshly ground pepper to taste

½	cup apple cider vinegar
1	pork tenderloin (about 2 pounds), butterflied; or a 4-pound pork shoulder cut in half, brined (see recipe on page 238)

1. Preheat the oven to 350 degrees.

2. Prepare the rub by combining the onion, garlic, thyme, rosemary, oil, red pepper flakes, black pepper, and vinegar in a bowl. Stir to mix well.

3. Remove the pork from the brine. Discard the brine.

4. On a half sheet pan with a rack, place the pork, and coat with the rub.

5. Place the pork in the oven on the lowest rack.

6. After 25 minutes, turn the pork over and cook for an additional 20 minutes, or until a meat thermometer registers 160 degrees.

7. Let the pork rest for 10 minutes before slicing and serving.

NOTE: If using a pork shoulder, for a crispy skin turn the broiler on high and place the pork under the flame until the desired color is achieved.

Pork Stew with Green Salsa and Fingerling Potatoes

Pork is one of my favorite meats. This dish was created by chef Rey's mother, Maria, and I just love it. She first made it for a dinner we hosted for Senator Barack Obama, and I loved it then. But it was my idea to add the heirloom fingerling potatoes, which I think makes it even better. This is a great buffet item that you can serve with warm tortillas. We make our tortillas fresh during our parties, but you could also buy high-quality tortillas and just cover them with foil and heat them.

Olive oil

4½ pounds pork butt

1½ onions, sliced

3 cloves garlic, minced

1 pound fingerling potatoes, sliced

1 quart pork or chicken stock

Salt and freshly ground black pepper to taste

Green Salsa

2 pounds tomatillos, peeled and cut in half

1 jalapeño pepper (or more for heat), cut in half and seeded

1 cup fresh cilantro

¼ cup warm water

1. Place a large Dutch oven over high heat and add some olive oil.

2. Add the pork and sauté until brown, about 15 minutes.

3. Remove the pork and set aside.

4. Add the sliced onions and sauté for 3 to 5 minutes while scraping the fond from the pork off the bottom of the pan.

5. Add the garlic and potatoes and sauté for 3 more minutes.

6. Return the pork to the pot and add the stock.

7. Bring to a boil for 10 minutes and then reduce the temperature to a steady simmer.

8. **Make the green salsa** in a blender by combining the tomatillos, jalapeño pepper, cilantro, and warm water. Blend well.

9. When the pork is fork-tender, add the green salsa and cook for 10 minutes more.

10. Season with salt and pepper. Serve warm.

Cuban-Asian Style Pork Rack

MAKES 15 SERVINGS

Instead of using the pork brine, I use the marinade. I let it sit for a day if possible in the refrigerator, or for at least two hours. This is another fabulous buffet party dish.

Marinade

12 cloves garlic, crushed

2 tablespoons crushed black peppercorns

2 tablespoons crushed red pepper

¼ cup chopped fresh thyme

¼ cup chopped fresh rosemary

3 bay leaves

2 cups white vinegar

½ cup ginger paste (fresh ginger peeled and grated)

¼ cup lemongrass, minced

½ cup fresh cilantro, crushed

1 cup kosher salt

4 tablespoons olive oil

2 pork racks

2 to 3 tablespoons olive oil

1. **For the marinade,** in a medium bowl, combine the garlic, black pepper, red pepper, thyme, rosemary, bay leaves, vinegar, ginger, lemongrass, cilantro, salt, and olive oil. Whisk to evenly blend. Pour over the pork and allow to marinate covered in the refrigerator overnight.

2. Remove the pork from the marinade.

3. Preheat the oven to 350 degrees.

4. **For the pork,** in a large Rondeau pan or large sauté pan, heat 2 to 3 tablespoons of olive oil over medium-high heat, and then sear the pork until it is golden brown on each side. Set it aside and repeat this step with the other rack.

5. Place the seared pork on a rack in a roasting pan lined with aluminum foil for an easy clean-up.

6. Cover the pork with foil and place in the oven for 30 minutes.

7. Check the temperature, rotate the rack, and cook for another 15 minutes, or until the internal temperature reaches 160 to 165 degrees.

8. Remove the pork and allow to rest 10 minutes before slicing.

Grilled Flank Steak

The secret to flank steak is to not overcook it, and to carve it on the bias, which makes it more tender.

1½ pounds flank steak (cut into 4 portions)

⅓ cup soy sauce

½ cup fresh orange juice

3 large cloves garlic, minced

1 tablespoon crushed red pepper

5 green onions, cut on the bias

2 tablespoons olive oil

Salt and freshly ground black pepper to taste

Flour or corn tortillas

1. Place the meat in a large bowl or a half sheet pan and set aside.

2. Combine the soy sauce, orange juice, garlic, red pepper, onions, oil, and salt and pepper. Mix well. Coat the meat with the soy sauce mixture. Cover with plastic, then place in the refrigerator for at least 1 hour.

3. While the meat is marinating, preheat the charcoal or gas grill. Be sure to oil the grates before placing the meat on the grill. A reversible flat top/grill top for the stove will work fine as well.

4. Place the meat on the grill, cooking it for 3 minutes on each side or to the temperature of your liking.

5. Remove the meat and let it rest on a plate for 10 minutes.

6. Set the oven to 200 degrees and place a stack of tortillas in the oven to warm. Slice the steak across the grain and serve with warm tortillas.

Jamaican Oxtail Stew

This is not a dish for anyone on a diet. It is for people who like to sit at a table and pick tender pieces of spicy meat off the bone. I find it easier and more enjoyable to pick up the bones and nibble on them, rather than using a knife. You leave too much delicious meat behind when you use a knife. I serve this dish with peas and rice.

2	tablespoons olive oil	1	red bell pepper, seeded and diced
6	oxtails	3	cloves garlic, minced
	Jamaican jerk seasoning for meat	2	tablespoons all-purpose flour
	All-purpose flour	1	jalapeño pepper, minced, seeded, and stemmed
1	onion, diced		
2	stalks celery, diced	1	teaspoon tomato paste
		2	quarts beef stock

1. Place a medium-sized Dutch oven over medium heat and add the olive oil.

2. While the oil is heating, season the oxtails with the Jamaican seasoning, and then dust them with all-purpose flour.

3. Place the oxtails in the Dutch oven and brown them for about 2 to 3 minutes on each side. I like to tie butcher's twine around each of the oxtails so they do not fall apart.

4. When browned, remove the oxtails and add the "holy trinity" (onion, celery, and bell pepper). Cook for 4 to 6 minutes, then add the minced garlic.

5. Add the flour to the pot and stir in the jalapeño pepper and tomato paste. Cook for 1 to 2 minutes.

6. Add 1 1/2 quarts of stock, stirring to blend. Save the remaining stock to add throughout the cooking process. This will cause the stock to thicken. You can add more stock if it is too thick.

7. Return the meat to the pot and bring to a boil for 5 minutes, then turn down to a slow simmer.

8. Cook the oxtail for 2 $^1/_2$ hours, or until the meat becomes very tender. Stir occasionally and add the remaining stock as necessary. When done, cut the twine and serve.

Yes, I have countless friends as family, but that little place that I could not run fast enough to get away from is calling me home.

—ART SMITH

Tequila-Lime Shrimp

MAKES 4 SERVINGS

We created this dish using Cielo, my friend's tequila. The tequila has a wonderful flavor and makes a great cocktail, but it is also great for marinating shrimp. These taste wonderful hot off the grill, and served at room temperature.

Marinade

1¼ cup tequila, divided

½ cup fresh lime juice

½ teaspoon cayenne pepper

1 tablespoon chili powder

1 jalapeño pepper, seeded and minced

Freshly ground black pepper to taste

¼ cup plus 1 tablespoon olive oil, divided

1 cup chopped fresh cilantro

Pinch of salt

2 pounds shrimp, peeled and deveined

1. **For the marinade,** combine ¼ cup of the tequila and the lime juice, cayenne pepper, chili powder, jalapeño, and black pepper in a medium bowl.

2. Toss the marinade over the shrimp, cover, and let marinate in the refrigerator for at least 30 minutes.

3. Remove from the refrigerator and toss the mixture with ¼ cup of the olive oil, the cilantro, and salt.

4. Place 1 teaspoon of olive oil in a large sauté pan over medium-high heat. When the oil begins to smoke, remove the pan from the stove and add 4 tablespoons of tequila to the pan. (You can avoid a dangerous flare-up by removing the pan from the stove.)

5. Drain the shrimp from the marinade. Discard the marinade. Toss one-quarter of the shrimp into the pan. Return the pan to the stove and cook for 1 to 2 minutes, tossing or stirring the shrimp.

6. Cook another 2 minutes and, using a slotted spoon or spatula, place the shrimp on a serving plate. Repeat the steps with the rest of the shrimp. Always remove the pan from the stove when tossing in the next batch of shrimp.

NOTE: This recipe can be cooked using presoaked wooden or metal skewers and placing them on the grill. It also can be done on a greased roasting pan in a 375 degree oven for 10 minutes. Be sure to stir the shrimp halfway through the cooking process for even cooking.

Steamed Clams with Chorizo and Fingerling Potatoes

MAKES 4 SERVINGS

This dish is based on a classic Portuguese recipe and was created by my friend chef Jason Handelman of Chicago's famed Fox & Obel market and cafe. If you're in the Chicago area, looking for the best ingredients to create the best dish, you can find them at this market.

2	tablespoon of extra virgin olive oil	4	cups washed little clams
4	cloves of garlic, mashed	1	cup sliced, cooked chorizo sausage
1	chile pepper, minced	2	tablespoons chopped Italian parsley plus some for garnish
2	cups bottled clam broth		Sea salt to taste
2	cups white wine		Freshly ground pepper
1	cup sliced fingerling potatoes		Zest of 1 lemon

1. Heat the olive oil in a Dutch oven over medium heat. Add the garlic and sauté until soft. Then add the minced chile. Pour in the broth and wine. Bring to a simmer. Add the potatoes and cook for 10 minutes, or until tender.

2. Add the clams and cook until they open. Remove from the heat, add the sausage, parsley, salt, and ground pepper, and stir carefully. Ladle into a bowl and top with lemon zest and more parsley. Serve with good bread.

Chile-Rubbed Leg of Lamb

MAKES 10 TO 12 SERVINGS

I created this dish for a holiday dinner, rubbing the lamb with chiles and allowing it to marinate for a couple of days beforehand. My wood-burning brick oven is great for roasting this dish, but it cooks just as well on a regular charcoal grill. Have your butcher bone the leg out for you and tie up the meat. This will make it easier to cook and serve, and for some strange reason it also makes the meat less gamey.

6	to 8 pounds boneless and tied leg of lamb, brined (see recipe on page 238)	6	cloves garlic, minced
¼	cup ground ancho chile powder (see pantry)	¼	cup chopped fresh thyme
½	cup mild ground chiles (see pantry)	¼	cup chopped fresh rosemary
		¼	cup chopped fresh parsley
		½	cup extra virgin olive oil

1. Preheat the oven to 350 degrees.

2. Remove lamb from the brine and discard the brine.

3. Combine the chile powder, chiles, garlic, thyme, rosemary, parsley, and oil in a medium bowl, mixing well. Rub the lamb with the herb mixture. Place the lamb in a lightly greased roasting pan with a rack.

4. Roast in the oven for 30 minutes, check the internal temperature, and then rotate the lamb.

5. Cook another 30 minutes before checking the temperature again. If the temperature is between 150 and 160 degrees, the lamb is medium. Remove it from the oven and let it rest for 10 minutes before slicing. If it is too rare, continue to cook to the desired temperature (170 degrees is well-done).

Anne Bloomstrand's Chicken Under a Brick

MAKES 2 SERVINGS

There are many recipes for this dish, but my beloved Annie B's is the best.

1	(3-pound) whole chicken, butterflied with the backbone removed	2	tablespoons chopped fresh parsley
	Salt and freshly ground black pepper	2	tablespoons chopped fresh oregano
¼	cup olive oil	2	tablespoons chopped fresh thyme
4	cloves garlic, minced		
2	tablespoons chopped fresh chives		

1. Lay the chicken on a baking sheet and bring to room temperature (approximately 20 minutes). Sprinkle with salt and pepper.

2. In a small bowl, make a paste by combining the olive oil, garlic, and the fresh herbs.

3. Loosen the skin on the chicken with your hands and spread the paste under the skin.

4. Place the chicken on the hot grill, skin side up.

5. Place a baking sheet on top of the chicken and weigh it down with a brick.

6. Close the grill and begin checking for doneness after 30 minutes. The chicken is done when a meat thermometer reads an internal temperature of 165 degrees.

7. When done, remove the brick, and then carefully remove the chicken from the grill on a baking sheet. (Caution—it will be hot!) Allow the chicken to rest 10 minutes before cutting and serving.

Barbecued Spare Ribs

I still remember the amazing barbecued pork chops I used to eat when I was a kid. They were served on white bread back then, and today I find it amusing that people love to eat around the bone once again.

Rub

¼ cup sweet paprika

4 tablespoons chili powder

1 tablespoon ground cumin

2 tablespoons dark brown sugar

Salt to taste

½ tablespoon ground red pepper

1 tablespoon dried oregano

1 tablespoon sugar

1 tablespoon freshly ground black pepper

½ teaspoon freshly ground white pepper

3 (3-pound) full slabs pork back ribs

2 cups wood chips, soaked in water overnight or for at least 2 hours

Your favorite barbecue sauce

1. **For the rub,** combine the paprika, chili powder, cumin, brown sugar, salt, red pepper, oregano, sugar, black pepper, and white pepper in a small bowl. Place the ribs on a large baking sheet. Sprinkle or rub both sides of the ribs with the dry rub. Let stand at room temperature for 1 hour or cover and refrigerate for up to 24 hours.

2. Drain water off the wood chips and place on an aluminum tray or a homemade tray of aluminum foil. Prepare an indirect-heat charcoal fire by putting all the coals in one corner or around the edges of the grill. Place the tray of chips above the hot coals. Close the lid and heat the grill to high until the chips are smoking (about 10 minutes).

3. Close the vents for medium heat.

4. Place the ribs in the center part of the grill where there are no coals. The temperature inside the grill should be 220 to 275 degrees.

5. Cover the grill and cook, turning every 30 minutes, until the meat starts to pull away from the bones, about 2 1/2 hours.

6. Remove the ribs and wrap them in heavy-duty aluminum foil. Set aside at room temperature for 1 hour.

7. Unwrap the ribs and brush them with barbecue sauce before serving.

Oven Barbecued Ribs

Barbecue may seem like a grueling job at times, but baking the meat in the oven creates wonderful results: intense flavor and falling-off-the-bone tenderness. You will love this recipe. Hopefully it will make you want to make barbecue more often.

Sauce

1   (16-ounce) bottle ketchup

1   cup brown sugar

¼   cup apple cider vinegar

2   teaspoons salt

3   teaspoons molasses

1   teaspoon lemon juice

1   teaspoon dry mustard

1   teaspoon minced fresh garlic

¼   teaspoon ground ginger

    Freshly ground black pepper

6   pounds baby back ribs, cut into 2-inch pieces

2   Vidalia onions, sliced

1. Preheat the oven to 350 degrees.

2. **For the sauce,** combine the ketchup, brown sugar, vinegar, salt, molasses, lemon juice, mustard, garlic, ginger, and black pepper in a medium bowl. Set aside.

3. Place the ribs in a lightly greased roasting pan. Cover with foil and bake for 90 minutes.

4. Remove the ribs from the oven and drain off any sauce, reserving for brushing and serving.

5. Dip or spread the ribs with the prepared sauce. Place the onions in a roasting pan, and then place the ribs on top of the onions. Cover and return the ribs to the oven.

6. Bake for another hour, brushing the ribs with the reserved sauce.

7. Remove the ribs from the oven and let rest for 10 minutes. Serve warm with any leftover sauce.

Bettye Jackson's Mississippi Chicken and Rice (Perlo)

MAKES 12 SERVINGS

Pam of Campfire Cafe gave me this recipe to prepare for my family reunion on our farm in Florida. I grew up with chicken and rice, and this is the "bee's knees" of recipes! I love you, Bettye and Pam, for sharing—thank you!

3	to 4 large, bone-in chicken breasts	1½	cups chopped celery
2	quarts chicken broth	1	teaspoon dried thyme leaves
½	cup (1 stick) unsalted butter	1	teaspoon hot red pepper flakes
1	pound smoked sausage links, cut into bite-size pieces	4	cups long-grain white rice
1	large white onion, chopped (about 1½ cups)		Salt and freshly ground black pepper to taste

1. Cover the chicken with water and boil in a large pot, uncovered, for 30 minutes.

2. Remove the chicken from the broth and reserve the broth.

3. When cool enough to handle, skin the chicken and remove the bones, pulling the meat from the bones. Cut the meat into bite-size pieces and set aside.

4. Melt the butter in a Dutch oven on top of the stove. Add the sausage, onion, and celery. Cook over medium heat until the onion starts to brown, about 10 minutes.

5. Add the seasonings and a little more salt than you might think is necessary.

6. Add the chicken, rice, and 1 quart of the reserved broth. Cover, bring to a simmer, and cook slowly without lifting the lid for 30 minutes. Serve hot with a green salad and corn bread.

Fried Chicken and Waffles

MAKES 8 TO 12 SERVINGS

This delicious recipe was inspired by my friend, food television personality Alton Brown. This is our most popular breakfast dish. We have served hundreds of these in my home kitchen. The dish takes some planning, but is so well worth it.

Another dear friend, Scott Peacock, taught me to brine my chicken, and I have done this ever since. I have had great results using cast iron pots by Staub, and I only use grapeseed oil. This oil is expensive but will not break down. You must remember to keep removing sediment from the oil. I like to fry dark meat first, and then proceed with the white. When cooking for a crowd, place fried chicken on a cooling rack instead of a sheet pan. You can finish the chicken in the oven, and test it with a food thermometer. The thermometer must come to 165 degrees.

2	gallons water	2	teaspoons cayenne pepper
1	cup kosher salt	2	teaspoons freshly ground black pepper
2	whole fryers, cut into 8 pieces		
1	gallon buttermilk	1	tablespoon garlic powder
¼	cup hot sauce	1	tablespoon Old Bay Seasoning
4	cups self-rising flour		Grapeseed oil for frying

1. Combine the water and salt and stir for a couple minutes to make a brine solution. Submerge the chicken pieces in the brine. Cover and refrigerate overnight.

2. Remove the chicken from the brine. Discard the brine and rinse the chicken. Combine the buttermilk and hot sauce. Pour over the chicken, cover, and marinate one more day in the refrigerator.

3. Combine the flour, cayenne pepper, black pepper, garlic powder, and Old Bay seasoning. Sift into a shallow dish to even out the spices.

4. Remove the chicken from the buttermilk and shake off as much buttermilk as possible.

5. Dredge a couple of pieces of chicken in the flour mixture, then dip in the buttermilk. Shake off the excess and dredge again in the flour. Repeat with the

Continued on next page

remaining chicken pieces. The chicken can be set on a tray for a short period, but fry it quickly so that the batter does not fall off.

6. Heat the oil to 375 degrees in a cast-iron skillet over high heat. Use a thermometer to make sure the oil is the correct temperature.

7. Using tongs, carefully lower the chicken into the hot oil, a few pieces at a time. Do not overcrowd the skillet. Allow the chicken to brown on one side for 6 to 7 minutes, and then turn over to the other side.

8. When cooked, carefully remove the chicken and drain on paper towels. Repeat with the remaining chicken. Serve warm with waffles.

Waffles

MAKES 12 (4-INCH) WAFFLES

Growing up in the South meant eating at the Waffle House, one of America's greatest roadside diners. I grew up eating waffles with cane syrup, but when I moved to the North I discovered people's love for maple syrup. Waffles are great for breakfast, but don't forget to serve them with fried chicken for supper now and then. This recipe will rock your world. Serve the waffles hot, with the fried chicken. Some people enjoy hot sauce and maple syrup together. We serve it just with maple syrup.

1¼ cups all-purpose flour	½ cup (1 stick) unsalted butter, melted
2 tablespoons sugar	
1 tablespoon baking powder	1 cup milk
½ teaspoon salt	3 large eggs, beaten

1. Lightly oil the grids of a waffle iron and heat.

2. Combine the flour, sugar, baking powder, and salt in a large bowl.

3. Make a well in the center and pour in the melted butter, milk, and eggs.

4. Whisk just until smooth. Do not overmix.

5. Spoon about ¼ cup of the batter into the center of each quadrant of the waffle iron and close it.

6. Cook until the waffles are golden brown, 3 to 4 minutes. Serve hot with fried chicken and maple syrup.

Coq au Vin

I especially love this classic French dish when it is made with white wine. It's a great dish for a party, and it's just fine to make it in advance.

2	tablespoons olive oil		2	cups chicken broth
2	slices thick-cut bacon, cut into pieces		1	cup dry white wine
1	whole chicken, cut into pieces		2	carrots, sliced
1	tablespoon chopped fresh thyme		1	cup frozen pearl onions, thawed
	Salt and freshly ground black pepper		1	turnip, peeled and cut into chunks
	Flour for dredging		1	bay leaf

1. In a Dutch oven over medium heat, add the olive oil. When hot, add the bacon pieces and fry until crisp, then remove and drain on paper towels.

2. Rub the chicken with the thyme and salt and pepper, then dredge in the flour.

3. Increase the heat to medium-high and add the chicken, browning on both sides. When you have browned all the chicken, pour off half of the fat.

4. Add the broth and white wine and reduce by one-half by simmering over medium-low heat for about 15 minutes.

5. Add the carrots, pearl onions, turnips, and bay leaf and simmer until the vegetables are tender.

6. When the chicken is tender, remove from the heat and cool. Remove and discard the bay leaf and serve immediately. This is also delicious served the following day.

Barbecue Worth Braggin' About
from Campfire Cafe™

MAKES 8 SERVINGS

In a world of fancy celebrity chefs, there is one great man, Johnny Nix, who has a heart for feeding people, and a love for cooking like no other person I have met. He cooked for our family reunion and made this wonderful pulled pork barbecue—the most superb barbecue I have ever eaten. Braised in Lodge cast-iron pots over an open fire for hours, this recipe produces tender shards of juicy pork perfect for sandwiches.

5	pounds boneless pork butt		½	cup brown sugar
¼	cup water		2	tablespoons molasses
1	large white onion, chopped		1	(28-ounce) can crushed tomatoes, undrained
1	jalapeño pepper, seeded and finely chopped		1	(16-ounce) can tomato paste
2	tablespoons olive oil		1	cup beef broth
2	tablespoons chili powder		2	bay leaves
½	teaspoon ground cumin			Small flour tortillas as needed
½	teaspoon ground coriander			White and red onion, very thinly sliced
½	teaspoon dried oregano			Bread and butter pickle slices
6	cloves garlic, minced			

1. In a 14-inch-deep Dutch oven, place the pork on a baker's rack or meat trivet.

2. Add ¼ cup of water to the bottom of the Dutch oven. Cover and cook over high heat for 20 minutes.

3. When the meat begins to cook, raise to a higher hook to reduce the heat, and cook for approximately 4 hours—low and slow.

4. When done, cool the meat and pull apart or shred. Set aside.

5. In a Dutch oven over medium heat, cook the onion and jalapeño pepper in the olive oil until just tender.

6. Add the chili powder, cumin, coriander, and oregano. Stir to mix. Add the garlic, brown sugar, molasses, tomatoes, tomato paste, beef broth, and bay leaves. Bring to a boil, cover, and simmer approximately 20 minutes until thickened. Remove the bay leaves.

7. Combine the meat and sauce. Serve wrapped in flour tortillas with pickles and onions on the side.

NOTE: To cook the pork in the oven, preheat the oven to 425 degrees. Cook the pork for 20 minutes in a roasting pan, then reduce the heat to 300 degrees and cook for 4 hours.

Cowboy Coffee from Campfire Cafe™

MAKES 4 SERVINGS

Coffee prepared over the open fire tastes like no other coffee. Johnny Nix taught me how to make this coffee for those rare occasions when I am roughing it. On your next family campout, you simply must make this coffee. And it's great with apple pie!

1   scoop coffee for every 2 cups water

1. Dump the coffee and water into a coffeepot.

2. Hang over the fire or over medium heat on the stove and bring to a low boil, then move to reduce the heat or lower the burner temperature to low.

3. Before 1 cup is poured, pour 1 cup of cold water down the coffeepot spout. This settles the grounds and replaces the cup that is served to keep the pot going for most of the day.

4. Add a few more scoops of coffee as needed throughout the day to keep it strong.

Sweet Ancho–Rubbed Tenderloin

MAKES 12 TO 15 SERVINGS

This will give your steak a Latin flavor that you will absolutely love. This rub can be used on any meat, poultry, game, or pork. (See photo on the bottom of page 199.)

¼	cup canola oil	8	cloves garlic, minced
5	dried ancho chiles	8	shallots, minced
½	cup light brown sugar		Salt to taste
¼	cup chopped Mexican chocolate		Freshly ground black pepper to taste
1	teaspoon salt		Olive oil for coating
		1	(6 pounds) whole beef tenderloin

1. Heat the canola oil in a deep sauté pan. When hot, add the chiles and fry for about 30 seconds each. Remove and place on paper towels to drain.

2. When slightly cooled, place the chiles in a blender. In a slow steady stream pour the same oil you used for frying into the blender while it runs. Add the brown sugar, chocolate, and salt. You want the mixture to be fairly coarse. Set aside while you prep the meat.

3. Combine the garlic, shallots, salt, pepper, and just enough olive oil to barely coat the meat. Rub over the tenderloin.

4. In a large, heavy saucepan or skillet over high heat, sear or grill the tenderloin for 10 minutes, turning frequently for even browning.

5. Preheat the oven to 350 degrees and allow the tenderloin to cool. Then cover with the chile mixture. Finish cooking the tenderloin to your preferred temperature in the oven.

6. Remove from the oven and allow to rest 10 minutes before slicing and serving.

Rib Roast

This holiday season I made a big beautiful rib roast for my friends and family.

First, you have to find a great meat purveyor. My friend Todd Hatoff of Allen Brothers in Chicago has the most beautiful prepared rib roast I have ever seen. It is superb! You can order it by mail or over the Internet. It arrives at your door and you take it from there. (Just remember, the cook is only as good as his or her ingredients.) I like to brine my roast the day before I roast it. This brings out the flavor and makes it more succulent. I love to serve my roast with some wonderful potatoes, such as the "Pommes Anna," which my friend Grant taught me how to make.

5   to 6 pounds rib roast, bone-in   ½   cup kosher salt
    (about 1 pound per person)
                                         1   cup crushed peppercorns
2   gallons water   (I use a mixture of colors)

1. Mix the water and salt together. Soak the roast in the brine overnight in the refrigerator.

2. The next day, remove the roast from the brine and discard the brine.

3. Preheat the oven to 350 degrees. Rub the crushed peppercorns all over the meat and place the meat in a roasting pan. Roast the meat for 2½ hours. Check the temperature every hour for preferred doneness (20 minutes per pound is standard).

4. Serve with Pommes Anna (see recipe on page 231).

Tilapia Wrapped in Banana Leaf

In Central America and other parts of the tropics, many dishes are wrapped in banana leaves, giving them a very special flavor. I get mine in the frozen foods sections of Latin American supermarkets here in Chicago. I also have a banana leaf tree in my kitchen, but I would shoot anyone who tried to cut a leaf from it.

Red Pepper Sauce

1	(8-ounce) jar roasted red peppers, drained
1	clove garlic
1	teaspoon dried oregano
¼	cup olive oil
	Salt and freshly ground black pepper to taste

1	bag frozen banana leaves, thawed and cut into 5- or 6-inch squares
8	(6 ounces each) tilapia fillets
	Salt and freshly ground black pepper to taste
	Olive oil

1. **For the red pepper sauce,** place the peppers, garlic, and oregano in a blender.

2. Puree while adding the olive oil in a steady stream. Season with salt and pepper. Transfer to a squeeze bottle or a bowl and set aside.

3. Preheat the oven to 350 degrees. Bring a large pot of salted water to a boil.

4. Blanch the banana leaves by plunging them into the boiling water for 1 minute. Remove and immediately submerge in ice water for 1 minute. Drain. Lay with the smooth side of the leaves up on a baking sheet lightly greased with olive oil.

5. Place each fillet skin side up on a banana leaf and season with salt and pepper. Fold each corner of the leaf over as if you were wrapping a gift. Flip the fish over *gently* so that the seam side is down.

6. Place the fish in the oven and cook for 20 minutes.

7. Remove from the oven and let rest for 5 minutes. Cut a slit across the top of the banana leaf, and drizzle or spoon the red pepper sauce over the fish. Serve hot.

Jambalaya for Company

Do you know what it's like to invite people over, and a dozen more than you expected show up? Well, at my house it happens a lot. I take it as a compliment because people who love good food spread the word. Here is one of my favorite "company" dishes that people always love. Make enough so that you have extra to either keep for yourself or send home with your guests.

2	tablespoons extra virgin olive oil	4	stalks celery, chopped
1	pound chicken thighs, cut into pieces	2	tablespoons Creole seasoning (see recipe on page 239)
1	pound shrimp, peeled and deveined	1	(6-ounce) can tomato paste
1	pound tilapia, white fish, halibut, or orange roughy, cut into cubes	4	tomatoes, peeled, seeded, and chopped
1	pound smoked sausage, sliced	8	cups chicken broth
1	large onion, chopped	2	bay leaves
1	bell pepper, chopped		Salt to taste
3	cloves garlic, minced	4	cups long-grain white rice
		1	cup chopped fresh Italian parsley

1. Place the olive oil in a large Dutch oven and place over medium heat. When hot, add the chicken, shrimp, fish, sausage, onion, bell pepper, garlic, and celery. Cook until just lightly brown.

2. Add the Creole seasoning, tomato paste, tomatoes, and chicken broth and bring to a boil.

3. Add the bay leaves, season with salt, and stir in the long-grain rice. Reduce the heat so that the mixture simmers, then cover. Cook until the liquid has almost evaporated, about 30 minutes. Great jambalaya should be a little wet.

4. Just before serving, remove the bay leaves and stir in the freshly chopped parsley. Serve and enjoy.

May you live as long as you want,
And never want as long as you live.
—TRADITIONAL IRISH BLESSING

ALL GREAT MEALS HAVE GREAT SIDE DISHES AS
part of the equation. Sometimes the sides become the meal itself. I can
remember many times not being able to decide which sides to order in
a restaurant, and solving that dilemma by ordering several sides and
skipping the entrée altogether! My chef Rey Villalobos' mother Maria
makes delicious Arroz Mexicana (Mexican Rice), which takes an
everyday meal and lifts it to another level. I love beans, too. Tuscan
beans cooked in a jar are so wonderful I could eat them once a week. I
serve them over rice when I have parties at my house, and guests always
adore them. Sides can be wonderfully healthy, like greens with smoked
turkey, or Swiss chard with bacon. Please do not forget about sides—
they can make a good meal great.

Mexican Arroz (Rice)

My life changed two years ago when I met Reymundo Villalobos, a talented young chef with immeasurable kindness and an old soul. He has blessed my life in so many ways that I can't begin to list them. We have cooked together for countless parties, and one of the greatest types of foods we prepare is Mexican cuisine. Rey's beloved mother Maria, whom everyone should meet, is the most wonderful Mexican cook I have ever met. Her rice is superb and we serve it at many meals.

1	clove garlic		Salt to taste
¼	onion, peeled	1½	quarts chicken stock
3	tomatoes, peeled, seeded, and chopped	¼	cup canola oil
		2	cups long-grain white rice

1. In a blender combine the garlic, onion, tomatoes, salt, and ½ cup of the chicken stock. Blend and set aside.

2. Heat the canola oil in a medium saucepan over medium-high heat. When hot, add the rice and fry until golden brown, 3 or 4 minutes.

3. Add the tomatoes and stir quickly. Add the remaining stock, stirring well.

4. Bring to a boil for 5 minutes and then reduce the heat and simmer for 15 minutes while covered. Do not uncover! Be patient!

5. After 15 minutes, turn off the heat and let the rice rest for 5 minutes. Stir and serve.

Tuscan Beans in a Jar

MAKES 8 TO 12 SERVINGS

This is authentic Italian comfort food. For anyone who has never tried it—this recipe is for you.

2	pounds Tuscan beans, soaked in water overnight in the refrigerator	2	quarts chicken or vegetable stock
10	Roma tomatoes	1	cup chopped fresh basil leaves
¼	pound pancetta, diced	¼	cup extra virgin olive oil
2	small onions, diced		Salt and freshly ground black pepper to taste

1. Drain the beans and rinse.

2. Bring a large pot of water to a boil and cut an *X* on the ends of the tomatoes. Drop the tomatoes into the water in batches, if necessary. After 40 seconds, remove and plunge into an ice-water bath. Leave in the ice water for 40 seconds and drain. The skins should peel right off. Cut the tomatoes in half lengthwise and remove the seeds.

3. Place a large Dutch oven over high heat, toss in the pancetta, and render until it begins to turn brown and crispy, 4 to 6 minutes.

4. Drain off some of the fat and toss in the onions, sautéing for 4 minutes, or until the onions begin to look translucent.

5. Reduce the heat to medium and add the beans, sautéing for about 5 minutes. Add the stock and bring to a boil. Reduce the heat to medium low and cook for 2½ hours.

6. When the beans are done, add the basil, olive oil, and salt and pepper. Serve immediately or let cool and then ladle into jars and refrigerate for later use. They will keep for up to three days.

Baked Beans on the Farm

MAKES 16 SERVINGS

These beans were made by chef Jason Handelman of Fox & Obel at my family picnic in Florida. At the end of the event there was not a single pot of beans to take home with us.

2	to 3 quarts water	1/3	cup maple syrup
2	pounds dried Great Northern white beans	1/2	cup molasses
		1/2	cup dark brown sugar
1	large onion, peeled	2	bay leaves
1	tablespoon plus 1 teaspoon kosher salt	1	tablespoon dry mustard
1/4	cup apple cider vinegar	1	teaspoon ground black pepper
1/8	teaspoon ground cinnamon	2	large onions, peeled and quartered
1/8	teaspoon ground cloves	1/4	pound salt pork (left whole, with the rind on)
1	tablespoon minced garlic		
1	cup ketchup or barbecue sauce	1/4	pound bacon (cut into 1/2-inch pieces)

1. In a large stockpot, add 2 quarts of water and bring to a boil over high heat. Add the dried beans and boil for 2 minutes (the water should cover the beans by at least 2 inches). Turn off the heat, cover, and let the beans soak for 1 hour.

2. Add 1 peeled onion and 1 teaspoon salt and bring to a boil again. Reduce the heat to low and simmer partially covered for 1½ to 2 hours, or until the beans are tender. Add more water if necessary—the water should always cover the beans.

3. Drain the beans and reserve the liquid. Discard the boiled onion. Add more water to the reserved cooking liquid, if necessary, to yield 2 quarts.

4. In a very large, deep bowl, combine the vinegar, cinnamon, cloves, garlic, ketchup, maple syrup, ¼ cup brown sugar, bay leaves, dry mustard, black pepper, boiled beans, and 2 quarts of the reserved liquid. Stir gently to thoroughly combine.

5. Place the other 2 onions (quartered) in the bottom of a lightly greased 4- to 5-quart bean pot, large Dutch oven, or 5-quart ovenproof baking dish, and pour the bean mixture over them.

6. Preheat the oven to 300 degrees.

7. Score the salt pork by cutting diagonal, crisscrossing slits about $^1/_2$ inch deep through the fatty side. Push the salt pork and cut bacon pieces into the beans.

8. Cover the pot tightly and bake in the middle of a 300-degree oven for 5 to 6 hours.

9. Check the beans during the cooking process, adding water as necessary and stirring occasionally.

10. Remove the lid and sprinkle the remaining $^1/_4$ cup of brown sugar evenly over the top of the hot bubbling beans. Bake uncovered for an additional hour.

11. Discard the bay leaves before serving.

Cowpeas with Bacon

MAKES 4 TO 6 SERVINGS

If you think you don't know what a cowpea is, think again. You probably know them by their other name, black-eyed peas. Although they're associated with the South, they're originally from Asia. Class dismissed!

2	cups cowpeas, soaked in water for at least 4 hours and up to 24 hours
1	pound bacon, diced
1	onion, diced
1½	quarts chicken or vegetable stock
	Salt and freshly ground black pepper to taste

Fried Shallots for Garnish

2	cups canola oil
1½	cups flour
1	teaspoon salt
½	teaspoon black pepper
4	shallots, sliced

1. Drain the beans from the soaking water and rinse with cold water. Set aside to drain.

2. Sauté the bacon in a Dutch oven over medium-high heat until it begins to crisp, 4 to 6 minutes.

3. Add the onion, sautéing until it becomes translucent, 2 to 4 minutes.

4. Add the drained beans and continue to cook for 5 minutes.

5. Add enough stock to cover the beans by 1½ inches. Season with salt and pepper and bring to a boil. Boil for 10 minutes, then reduce the heat to a steady simmer for 1½ to 2 hours.

6. Check the beans, making sure they still have some firmness to them.

7. **For the garnish,** in a sauté pan, add the canola oil and place over medium-high heat.

8. In a mixing bowl, combine the flour, salt, and pepper.

9. Dredge the shallots in the flour, dusting off any excess.

10. Add a ring of shallots to the hot oil to check that they do not brown too quickly.

11. Adjust the heat as necessary and add the remaining shallots to the oil. Drain on a paper towel and cool. Garnish the bowl of beans with the fried shallots. Enjoy!

Red Beans and Rice

MAKES 6 SERVINGS

I loved eating this dish while I traveled through the Caribbean islands. The coconut milk makes it very unusual, and I love the jalapeño and thyme seasoning.

2	tablespoons extra virgin olive oil	1	(15-ounce) can red beans, drained and rinsed
1	onion, minced	1½	cups coconut milk
1	jalapeño pepper, seeded and minced	1	cup chicken broth
2	cups uncooked white basmati rice	1	sprig fresh thyme
			Salt and freshly ground black pepper to taste

1. In a Dutch oven over medium-high heat, add the olive oil and onion and cook until soft, then add the jalapeño pepper.

2. Add the rice and cook for 5 minutes.

3. Add the beans, coconut milk, and chicken broth and bring to a boil. Reduce the heat to low, and add the thyme and salt and pepper. Cook until the broth and coconut milk are reduced, about 25 minutes. Ladle into individual bowls and serve hot.

Black Beans and Rice

This wonderful creation is a favorite with Cuban Americans. I spent a lot of time in Miami and remember enjoying this dish in South Beach.

1	pound dried black beans, soaked in water overnight in the refrigerator
½	pound smoked ham hock, chopped
1	onion, chopped
1	clove garlic, minced
1½	cups uncooked white basmati rice

2	quarts chicken broth
1	sprig fresh thyme
1	bay leaf
	Salt and freshly ground black pepper to taste
½	onion, chopped for garnish
1	tomato, chopped for garnish

1. Drain the beans and put them in a Dutch oven. Cover with fresh water and cook over medium-high heat for 1 hour or until tender.

2. Drain, return the beans to the Dutch oven, and add the chopped ham hock, onion, and garlic. Cook until soft, about 5 minutes.

3. Add the rice and cook 5 minutes longer. Add the broth, thyme, and bay leaf and season with salt and pepper. Cover and reduce the heat to low. Cook until the liquid is absorbed and the rice is tender, about 25 minutes.

4. Remove the bay leaf and serve with chopped onion and tomato.

Maria's Beans Borracho (Drunken Beans)

MAKES 8 SERVINGS

You've never tasted beans like this—trust me.

1	pound pinto beans		1	large onion, diced
1	teaspoon salt		1	(12-ounce) bottle full-flavored beer
1	pound bacon, diced			
½	jalapeño pepper, seeded and diced		¼	cup chopped fresh cilantro

1. In a medium stockpot, add the beans and cover them with 3 inches of water.

2. Bring to a boil, then reduce heat to bring to a steady simmer. Cook for 3 hours or until the beans are tender, then add salt and set aside.

3. In a large Dutch oven over high heat, add the bacon and cook for 6 minutes, draining excess fat.

4. Add the jalapeño pepper and onion and cook for 3 minutes. Add the beans, half of the stock from the beans, and the beer. Bring to a boil, then add the cilantro. Serve hot.

Asian Pressure Cooker Risotto

MAKES 6 SERVINGS

I absolutely love pressure cooker risotto. What's great is that you can have a perfect risotto in seven minutes. You can add all kinds of ingredients and it will always come out great.

2   tablespoons extra virgin olive oil

1   onion, chopped

1   clove garlic, minced

2   cups Arborio rice

4   cups chicken broth, hot

1   cup frozen soybeans, thawed

2   cups fresh spinach

1   cup bean sprouts

1/2   cup grated Parmesan cheese

1/4   cup chopped fresh basil

1/4   cup cream

2   tablespoons unsalted butter

Salt and freshly ground black pepper to taste

1. Combine the olive oil, onion, and garlic in a pressure cooker over medium heat. Cook for 5 minutes. Add the rice and cook another 5 minutes.

2. Add the heated broth and cover. Cook for about 7 minutes, or whatever the manufacturer's directions say.

3. Remove from the heat and stir in the soybeans, spinach, sprouts, cheese, basil, cream, and butter. Season with salt and pepper and serve immediately.

Greens with Smoked Turkey

MAKES 4 TO 6 SERVINGS

Greens—my favorite vegetable from the South. As I studied cooking I found that mixing different types of greens together made the dish even tastier. My cooking friend, singer Patty LaBelle, taught me this trick and you will love it!

3	tablespoons extra virgin olive oil	1	(1 to 1½-pound) smoked bone-in turkey, cut in pieces
1	onion, chopped	8	cups chicken broth
1	stalk celery, chopped	5	pounds fresh mixed greens (for example: turnip greens, collards, mustard greens, and chard), washed and dried
1	bell pepper, seeded and chopped		Vinegar to taste
1	clove garlic, minced		
1	jalapeño pepper, seeded and minced		

1. Combine the olive oil, onion, celery, bell pepper, and garlic in a large Dutch oven over medium-high heat. Cook until tender.

2. Add the jalapeño pepper, turkey, and chicken broth and bring to a boil.

3. Add the greens and reduce the heat to simmer. Cover and cook for 1 hour, or until the greens are tender. Serve warm with vinegar.

Sautéed Spinach with Meyer Lemon Zest

MAKES 4 SERVINGS

There's nothing wrong with a classic wilted spinach dish, but this is my recipe for a new and improved version.

1½ tablespoons extra virgin olive oil

½ small white onion, diced

1 shallot, minced

1 clove garlic, minced

1 tablespoon Meyer lemon zest

2 pounds baby spinach

1 Meyer lemon, juiced

Salt and freshly ground black pepper to taste

1. Place a large sauté pan over medium-high heat and add the olive oil. When hot, add the onion and cook until translucent, 1 to 3 minutes.

2. Add the shallot and garlic, cooking 1 minute and stirring constantly.

3. Add the lemon zest and spinach, cooking 1 to 2 minutes, or until the spinach wilts.

4. Add the lemon juice and sauté for 1 more minute. Season with salt and pepper and serve immediately.

Roasted Brussels Sprouts

These tiny relatives of cabbage have a delightful bitter tinge to them. When picking out Brussels sprouts, remember that the smaller they are, the more tender they will be.

2 pounds Brussels sprouts, peeled, trimmed, and halved

4 cloves garlic, minced

Olive oil for lightly coating

1 teaspoon red pepper flakes

Salt and freshly ground black pepper to taste

1. Preheat the oven to 325 degrees.

2. Place the Brussels sprouts and garlic in a bowl. Slowly add the olive oil while tossing to lightly coat.

3. Arrange the Brussels sprouts out on a baking sheet and sprinkle with the red pepper flakes and salt and pepper.

4. Roast in the oven for 10 minutes. Remove and cover with foil. Return the Brussels sprouts to the oven and roast 10 to 15 more minutes. Serve warm.

Swiss Chard with Bacon

MAKES 4 SERVINGS

This is another variation on wilted spinach. The addition of bacon and the substitution of Swiss chard makes this a heartier version of the original salad. Sometimes I mix the two kinds of chard together: Swiss chard and ruby chard. The ruby chard has vibrant red stalks and a deep red and greenish leaf. Swiss chard has very dark green leaves and a silvery stalk.

1½ tablespoons olive oil	2 to 3 bunches Swiss chard, washed, rinsed, and with stems removed
1 small onion, diced	Salt and freshly ground black pepper to taste
2 cloves garlic	
8 slices bacon, chopped	

1. In a large sauté pan over medium heat, add the olive oil. When hot, add the onions and cook 2 to 4 minutes.

2. Add the garlic and bacon, cooking another 2 minutes.

3. Roll up the chard leaves and slice. This type of cut is called "chiffonade."

4. Add the chard to the pan. Because it is a little more firm than spinach, it will take longer to cook. Cover and cook 4 to 6 minutes. Season with salt and pepper. Serve immediately.

Grilled Zucchini and Yellow Squash

A side of winter vegetables adds flavor and texture to any meal. Color, too! Slice each squash long enough so they do not fall through the grates of the grill.

4	cloves garlic, minced	3	zucchini, sliced
1	teaspoon chopped fresh thyme	3	yellow squash, sliced
1	teaspoon chopped fresh rosemary		Salt and freshly ground black pepper to taste
	Olive oil for coating		

1. In a small saucepan over low heat, add the garlic, chopped herbs, and olive oil.

2. Cook for 3 to 6 minutes, stirring occasionally. This will help release the flavor of each ingredient. While cooking, prepare a hot grill.

3. Arrange the squash on a baking sheet and brush each side with the flavored oil.

4. Transfer the vegetables to the hot grill, cooking each side 1 to 2 minutes. This should be enough time for each piece to show beautiful grate marks. Remove from the grill and season with salt and pepper. Serve warm.

Grilled Fingerling Potatoes

These little potatoes pick up a huge amount of flavor from the grill. They also acquire a delightfully subtle crunch when they begin to char.

2   pounds fingerling potatoes, halved

3   tablespoons olive oil

Salt and freshly ground black pepper to taste

1. Bring a large pot of water to a boil and add 2 tablespoons of salt.

2. Add the potatoes and cook for 4 to 5 minutes. Remove the potatoes immediately after cooking so they don't overcook. Drain and run under cold water to stop the cooking process.

3. Meanwhile, prepare the grill. When the potatoes are cool enough to handle, place them in a bowl and toss with the olive oil and salt and pepper.

4. Place the potatoes on the grill, moving them as little as possible.

5. When you begin to see char marks, remove and serve.

Skin-On Mashed Potatoes (3 of a Kind)

MAKES 4 TO 6 SERVINGS

Sometimes we forget how great potato skins taste. This recipe helps us remember.

1	pound Yukon gold potatoes, unpeeled	1½	cups half-and-half
1	pound red potatoes, unpeeled	¼	cup butter
1	pound fingerling potatoes, unpeeled		Salt and freshly ground black pepper to taste

1. Bring a large pot of water to a boil and add 2 tablespoons salt.

2. Place the potatoes in the pot and cook for 10 minutes, or until tender.

3. In a small saucepan over low heat, add the half-and-half and the butter. Heat until the butter is melted, stirring constantly.

4. When the potatoes are completely tender, drain and return to the pot.

5. While mashing the potatoes with a potato masher, add the half-and-half and butter mixture a little at a time. (Adding small amounts of liquid at a time will prevent runny mashed potatoes.)

6. Season with salt and pepper and serve warm.

Iron Skillet Vegetables

MAKE 4 SERVINGS

My friends at Campfire Cafe, came to my family's reunion on our historic farm in Jasper, Florida. We built campfires, and cooked pulled pork, and chicken and rice. Johnny Nix came up with this wonderful seasonal vegetable side dish. We gathered local produce and made this great dish. On your next camping trip don't forget the vegetables.

2	tablespoons extra virgin olive oil	1	cup green beans
1	small onion, chopped	1	bell pepper, green, yellow or red cut into slices
2	cloves garlic, mashed	1	teaspoon dried basil
1	cup broccoli flowerettes		Salt to taste
1	cup peeled and sliced carrots		Fresh ground black pepper

1. Heat the olive oil in a preheated seasoned cast-iron skillet over medium heat—on the stove or over the fire. Add the onion and cook until soft, about 2 minutes. Add the garlic and cook for 2 minutes.

2. Add the broccoli, carrots, green beans, and bell pepper and toss to coat the vegetables with the oil. Cook until the vegetables are tender, about 5 minutes. Add the basil and season with salt and freshly ground black pepper. Serve immediately.

Herb-Roasted Potatoes

MAKES 4 SERVINGS

You can never have enough potato recipes because potatoes are so versatile and so easy to prepare.

1½ pounds red potatoes or 1 pound Yukon gold potatoes

¼ cup chopped fresh thyme

¼ cup chopped fresh rosemary

¼ cup chopped fresh oregano

¼ cup chopped fresh chives

¼ cup chopped fresh parsley

¼ cup olive oil

4 cloves garlic, minced

Salt and freshly ground black pepper to taste

1. Preheat the oven to 350 degrees.

2. Rinse the potatoes and drain. I like to leave the skin on for color and texture.

3. Quarter each potato and place in a large bowl, tossing with the herbs, olive oil, and garlic.

4. Lightly grease a baking sheet and arrange the potatoes in a single layer.

5. Sprinkle with salt and pepper, then place in the oven.

6. Roast for 20 minutes, then remove from the oven and move the potatoes around with a spatula to prevent sticking.

7. Return to the oven for 15 more minutes. Check for tenderness. Serve warm.

Okra Fritters

I created these wonderful fritters for a party at the Hudsons' beautiful home in Pensacola, Florida. Everyone in the South loves okra, and this is a great way to serve this slimy vegetable. Don't fear the slime!

1	onion, minced	1	cup cornmeal
½	bell pepper, minced	½	cup self-rising flour
1	stalk celery, minced		Salt and freshly ground black pepper to taste
1	jalapeño pepper, seeded and minced	1	pound fresh okra, sliced
1	cup buttermilk		Grapeseed oil for frying
4	eggs, beaten		

1. In a large bowl, combine all the onion, bell pepper, celery, jalapeño pepper, buttermilk, eggs, cornmeal, flour, and salt and pepper.

2. Gently fold in the okra. Do not overmix or the okra will become excessively sticky.

3. In a cast-iron skillet, add enough grapeseed oil to fill halfway. Place over medium-high heat.

4. When the oil is hot, drop little spoonfuls of fritter batter into the oil and fry until the fritters are crispy and brown. Drain on paper towels and serve with a sprinkling of salt.

Chicken and Okra Gumbo

This Creole stew is wonderful served with freshly cooked white rice. I love to make it for friends who are feeling a little under the weather.

1	whole chicken (about 4 pounds)
2	onions, chopped
4	stalks celery, chopped
1	bell pepper, chopped
2	cloves garlic, minced
1	(15-ounce) can diced tomatoes
2	sprigs thyme
1	bay leaf
4	cups chopped fresh okra
	Salt and freshly ground black pepper to taste
	Hot sauce to taste

1. In a large pot over medium-high heat, add the chicken and cover with water.

2. Add the onions, celery, bell pepper, and garlic and simmer for 20 minutes.

3. Remove the chicken from the pot and allow it to cool.

4. When the chicken is cool enough to handle, remove the skin and bones. Shred the meat and set aside.

5. Add the tomatoes, thyme, bay leaf, and okra to the broth in the pot. Simmer for 5 minutes.

6. Add the shredded chicken to the pot. Season with salt, pepper, and a dash of hot sauce. Just before serving, remove the bay leaf.

Corn Pudding

This delicious savory pudding is perfect with the holiday turkey and other poultry. I love it with a little Parmesan cheese.

1	(14-ounce) can evaporated milk	1	(15¼-ounce) can whole kernel corn, drained
1	cup heavy cream	1	(15-ounce) can creamed corn
4	eggs	½	onion, minced and sautéed
	Salt and freshly ground black pepper to taste	½	cup grated Parmesan cheese

1. Grease a 5 x 7-inch casserole dish and set aside. Preheat the oven to 300 degrees.

2. In a large bowl, beat the milk, cream, and eggs. Season with salt and pepper.

3. Add the corn, creamed corn, sautéed onion, and Parmesan cheese.

4. Pour into the prepared casserole dish, then place the casserole dish in a baking pan, adding boiling water to make a *bain-marie*, or water bath. This will prevent the custard from curdling.

5. Place in the oven and bake for 45 minutes, or until set. Serve immediately.

Chicken and Dumplings

These lovelies are made throughout the South and the Midwest. Some folks' dumplings are fluffy, and some are like fine pasta. My mother makes a mean chicken and dumplings. It is so soothing— great for when you are feeling a little under the weather. Select a high-quality fresh chicken and simmer it to bring out all the great chicken flavor possible. The secret to this dish is a great broth.

Broth

1 whole chicken, 4 to 5 pounds

1 onion, chopped

1 stalk celery, chopped

Dumplings

2 cups all-purpose flour

1 egg, beaten

2 tablespoons canola oil

Pinch of salt

Chopped fresh parsley for garnish

Kosher salt and freshly ground black pepper to taste

1. **For the broth,** in a Dutch oven over medium heat, place the chicken, enough water to cover, the onion, and the celery. Bring to a low simmer and cover. Skim the residue off the top as it cooks. Make sure you never reduce the simmer or the broth will not be clear.

2. When the chicken is tender, remove it from the broth and allow the chicken to cool. When it is cool, remove the skin and bones, cut the chicken into pieces, and set aside.

3. Keep the broth warm while you make the dumplings.

4. **For the dumplings,** pour the flour into a large bowl and make a well in the center. Add the egg, oil, and salt. Using a fork, mix the ingredients together.

5. Transfer the dough to a lightly floured surface and knead 5 times.

6. Roll out the dough to $1/4$-inch thick and cut into strips with a sharp knife or a pastry wheel. Place on a sheet pan and refrigerate. My mother, Addie Mae, puts hers in the freezer because she likes them very firm.

7. Increase the heat of the broth to medium-high. Add the dumplings one at a time, but *do not stir.*

8. As you drop in the dumplings, take a spoon and pour the hot broth over them, then add another layer of dumplings. When all the dumplings are in the pot, reduce the heat to a simmer and cook the dumplings until tender.

9. Just before serving, add the cooked chicken and season with salt and pepper. Garnish with chopped parsley and serve warm.

Pommes Anna

MAKES 4 SERVINGS

1½ pounds russet potatoes

4 tablespoons unsalted butter, melted

2 cups mashed potatoes

2 ounces soft goat cheese

2 tablespoons chives

Salt to taste

1. Preheat the oven to 425 degrees.

2. Peel the potatoes, and slice them very thin. Place them in a large bowl of cold water and let them soak for 3 to 5 minutes. Drain the potatoes, pat them dry, and arrange them on paper towels to continue to dry.

3. Generously brush the bottom and sides of a 9-inch nonstick skillet with the melted butter. Brush each potato slice with butter.

4. Arrange the potato slices in a layer, overlapping them slightly, in the skillet.

5. Add the mashed potatoes, goat cheese, and chives and spread across the bottom. Season with salt.

6. Repeat with another layer of potato slices and another layer of mashed potatoes, goat cheese, chives, and salt and continue layering until the potatoes are all used.

7. Cover the skillet with buttered foil and bake in the middle of the oven for 30 minutes. Remove the foil and bake another 25 minutes. When the potatoes are tender, remove the skillet. Gently invert the potatoes onto a serving plate and serve immediately.

May you have warm words on a cold evening,
A full moon on a dark night,
And the road downhill all the way to your door.
—TRADITIONAL IRISH BLESSING

Menu

Eggs Rancheros

Chili Rubbed Lamb

Pork

BRINES ADD FLAVOR AND MOISTURE TO FOOD.

One secret to making a great brine is to use only kosher salt or sea salt. Along with using natural salt, other aromatics can be added: sugar, peppercorns, garlic, vinegars, herbs, and a bay leaf—pretty much anything you like.

Cultures all over the world rely on aromatics to create flavor. The American South uses its "holy trinity" for everything, and the French would not think of making a sauce without a mirepoix. The Spanish and Italians make a paste of vegetables called sofrito and add it to their dishes. Aromatics, no matter what they are called by certain cultures, are one of the fundamentals of cooking, and a proven way to add flavor.

Brine for Turkey

Every year without fail, dozens of people ask me how to make a perfect turkey. The number one rule is to brine the bird before you cook it.

2	cups kosher salt	3	bay leaves
½	cup sugar	3	cloves garlic, crushed
2	tablespoons roughly cracked black peppercorns	2	to 3 sprigs of rosemary

1. Place the salt, sugar, peppercorns, bay leaves, garlic, and a cup of cold water into a saucepan over medium-high heat. Stir until all of the salt and sugar has dissolved. Remove from the heat and cool to room temperature.

2. When brining you want to use a large nonreactive pot or a plastic container and completely submerge your turkey in cold water. Place plates on top of the turkey so that it does not float to the top.

3. Add the brine and refrigerate for 6 to 24 hours.

Brine for Chicken

MAKES 1¼ CUPS BRINE

It may seem strange to brine chicken for frying, but the results are amazing. Years ago I worked for Colonel Sanders Kentucky Fried Chicken, and sure enough, they brined all of their chicken. They called it "marinating" in those days, but it was brining, which produces moist, succulent chicken. My southern cooking colleague Scott Peacock started me down the brining road way back when. His chicken is terrific, and when you are in Atlanta, you simply must visit his restaurant, Water Shed.

1	cup kosher salt	2	bay leaves
¼	cup sugar	1	tablespoon black peppercorns
5	cloves garlic		

1. Place the salt, sugar, garlic, bay leaves, peppercorns, and 2 cups cold water into a saucepan over medium-high heat. Stir constantly until the sugar and salt dissolve. Remove from the heat and cool to room temperature.

2. When brining chicken use a nonreactive pot or a plastic container. Completely submerge the poultry in cold water and weigh it down with a plate. Add the brine and cover.

3. Let the chicken sit in the brine for at least 2 hours, preferably overnight.

Brine for Pork or Lamb

MAKES 6^{1}/$_{2}$ CUPS BRINE

It's good to brine pork for at least one day, so allow for enough time. This will help to tenderize and add flavor to this large piece of meat.

2	cups kosher salt	4	cups apple cider vinegar
½	cup sugar	12	cloves garlic, crushed
2	tablespoons black peppercorns	1	onion, cut in half
3	bay leaves		

1. Place the salt, sugar, peppercorns, bay leaves, vinegar, garlic, and onion in a large saucepan over medium-high heat.

2. Stir until all of the salt and sugar has dissolved. Remove from the heat and cool to room temperature.

3. When brining pork use a nonreactive pot or a plastic container. Completely submerge the pork in cold water. Weigh the pork down with a plate. Add the brine and refrigerate for 6 to 24 hours.

Art's Homemade Creole Seasoning

MAKES ¼ CUP

There are many seasonings on the shelves these days, and sadly they are heavy in salt and chemicals. Well, there is light at the end of the seasoning tunnel. Here is my quick recipe that is one of the keys to the seasoning kingdom. Enjoy!

2	teaspoons cayenne pepper	1	tablespoon dried oregano
1	tablespoon ground black pepper	1	tablespoon dried thyme
1	tablespoon white pepper		

1. Place the cayenne pepper, black pepper, white pepper, oregano, and thyme in a spice bottle.

2. Shake well and keep in a cool, dark place. It's best to make small amounts.

Holy Trinity

This is the base of a lot of southern cooking—from soups and sauces to roasted pork, chicken, and beef. My mother keeps this aromatic in her refrigerator. I always add garlic to my holy trinity. I use fresh garlic, never the dry ground stuff—just ask my sous chef Rey.

3	stalks celery, diced	1	green bell pepper, diced
1	onion, diced	3	cloves garlic, minced

Keep the vegetables separated and sealed in plastic containers or zip-top bags to keep fresh. I like to keep plenty on hand at all times, for whenever I do a lot of cooking. The way I prepare it is adding 1 tablespoon of butter to a skillet over medium heat and saute the onions until translucent. Add the celery, pepper, and garlic and cook until soft.

Mirepoix

The French use this aromatic as a base for almost all of their cooking, including braised meats, soups, and sauces. Keep all the vegetables separated in small containers or plastic zip-top bags until you are ready to make mirepoix.

1	tablespoon olive oil	3	celery stalks, diced
1	onion, diced	3	cloves garlic, minced
1	carrot, peeled and diced		

1. Place the olive oil in a large sauté pan over medium heat.

2. Add the onion and cook for 4 to 6 minutes while stirring. The onion will begin to turn clear.

3. Add the carrot and cook for another 4 minutes while stirring.

4. Add the celery and garlic and cook for another 4 minutes.

NOTE: When making brown sauces, make sure the mirepoix has a caramelized color.

Sofrito

I like to use this when I need to add some spice to my life. Chef Rey adds this to many of his dishes because he loves food with just a little kick to it. Spanish **sofrito** *usually consists of rendered pork fat with annatto seed fried for color, then removed from the pan and added to the rest of the base. Rey and I add jalapeño or serrano peppers to our* **sofrito** *for that wonderful flavor. We also use olive oil instead of rendered pork fat. This aromatic is used for soups, sauces, rubs for meats and poultry, and also for frying rice.*

1	tablespoon olive oil	1	red bell pepper, seeded and diced
1	onion, diced	½	jalapeño pepper, seeded and minced
1	green bell pepper, seeded and diced	3	cloves garlic, minced

1. Add the olive oil to a sauté pan and place over medium heat. When hot, add the onion and cook 4 to 6 minutes or until the onion turns clear.

2. Add the peppers and garlic. Cook for another 4 to 6 minutes or until soft.

NOT EVERY CHEF IS ABLE TO BAKE WELL, BUT I
happen to love baking and find it to be extremely easy. All you have to
do is follow directions and let everything fall (or hopefully rise) into
place. My guests love the smell of fresh bread being baked when they
enter my house. My foccacia, I believe, is one of the best recipes I have
ever created, and people ask for it over and over again. When we met
for our first meeting to talk about this book, my co-editor Michael
Austin arrived bearing a loaf of Irish soda bread he had baked using his
mother's recipe. It not only won me over but also our entire team.
Bread is simple, as you will see, and you will find yourself making it
over and over. Pizza dough, like bread, is best when it is homemade.
I especially adore a thin crust pizza, and even a thicker one as long as
the dough is crispy on the bottom. I have found that the secret to
making great pizza dough is to refrigerate it overnight. This ensures
that the dough will not overproof, and will have great flavor and body.
I love pizza so much that I put a wood-fire brick oven in my back
courtyard. We fire it up to make pizza appetizers for guests at just about
every party we throw, but a simple pizza stone in your oven will give you
very similar results.

Basic Focaccia Recipe

Focaccia has become a huge part of my repertoire. I love the texture and all the goodies that give it such great flavor. Once you try this, you will make it over and over again.

1¼ packages active dry yeast

1 cup warm water (105-115 degrees)

1 teaspoon honey

¼ cup olive oil

1½ teaspoons salt

3 cups unbleached flour as needed

1. Combine the yeast with ¼ cup of warm water and the honey in the mixing bowl of a heavy duty stand mixer and stir gently.

2. Let the yeast rest, 10 to 15 minutes.

3. Add the remaining water, add the oil and salt.

4. Attach the mixer's paddle and set on low speed while adding flour until you have soft dough. Mix for about 4 minutes.

5. Replace the paddle turn with a dough hook, set the mixer on medium-high speed, and knead for another 10 minutes, or until the dough is smooth.

6. Preheat the oven to 350 degrees.

7. Roll out the dough to fit a half sheet pan or 9-inch pie pan or casserole. Place the dough in the baking pan or dish and press down on the dough with your fingertips, making indentations.

8. Bake in the oven for 30 to 45 minutes, checking periodically to make sure it does not overcook.

9. Once the color has reached a golden brown, remove and let cool. Cut into wedges and serve hot or cold.

Focaccia with Goat Cheese and Herbs

MAKES 8 TO 12 SERVINGS

Years ago, Dr. Jerry Kadis gave me homemade goat cheese from his herd of goats on his Thomasville Farm. I have loved goat cheese ever since then. I later discovered that it is great on focaccia.

1¼ packages active dry yeast

1 cup warm water (105-115 degrees)

1 teaspoon honey

1/4 cup olive oil

1½ teaspoon salt

3 cups unbleached flour as needed

6 ounces goat cheese, crumbled

2 tablespoons chopped fresh rosemary

1 tablespoon chopped fresh thyme

1 tablespoon chopped fresh basil

2 tablespoons chopped fresh parsley

Olive oil for drizzling

Salt and freshly ground black pepper to taste

1. Combine the yeast with ¼ cup of warm water and the honey in the mixing bowl of a heavy duty stand mixer and stir gently.

2. Let the yeast rest, 10 to 15 minutes.

3. Add the remaining water, add the oil and salt.

4. Attach the mixer's paddle and set on low speed while adding flour until you have soft dough. Mix for about 4 minutes.

5. Replace the paddle turn with a dough hook, set the mixer on medium-high speed, and knead for another 10 minutes, or until the dough is smooth.

6. Preheat the oven to 350 degrees.

7. In a half sheet pan, press down on the dough with your fingertips, making indentations.

8. Spread the dough evenly in the pan, then drizzle it with olive oil.

9. Combine the goat cheese and herbs and crumble over the top of the focaccia as evenly as possible, then drizzle more olive oil over the top.

10. Bake in the oven for 30 to 45 minutes, checking periodically to make sure it does not overcook.

11. Once the color has reached a golden brown, remove and let cool. Cut into wedges and serve hot or cold.

No Knead Multigrain Bread

In my first book I did an easy "no knead cheese bread" and it was a huge hit. Here is a healthier bread recipe that your family will love. I love to make it to serve at home, and it always disappears quickly. On the rare occasion I have any stale pieces, I put them in my frittata.

1 (¼-ounce) package active dry yeast	2 tablespoons unsalted butter, melted
1½ cups warm water, 100 to 110 degrees	1 teaspoon salt
2 cups all-purpose flour	1 cup whole wheat flour
2 tablespoons honey	½ cup uncooked mixed grain cereal (see pantry)

1. In a large bowl, combine the yeast and warm water, stirring until yeast dissolves. Allow to bubble. It should begin to activate in about 15 minutes.

2. Add the flour, honey, unsalted butter, and salt. Mix well.

3. Add the whole wheat flour and the cereal, mixing well.

4. Place a towel over the top of the bowl and place the bowl away from drafts. Allow the dough to double in bulk. Punch down.

5. Lightly grease a standard loaf pan. Place the dough into the pan. Cover and allow it to double in size once more.

6. Preheat the oven to 375 degrees. When doubled, bake for 35 to 40 minutes. (A great way to tell if the loaf is ready is to tap on it. If it sounds hollow, it's ready!)

7. Remove from the oven and the pan. Allow the loaf to cool on a wire rack before slicing.

Yogurt Cheddar Biscuits

MAKES 1 DOZEN SMALL BISCUITS

I created these fabulous biscuits on the spot one evening for a dinner. My friends love them, and they are easy to make. I prefer to roll them by hand and place them close together. Make some extras to save for later!

2 cups self-rising flour	¼ cup grated sharp cheddar cheese
¼ cup (½ stick) unsalted butter, cold and cut into pieces	½ cup plain yogurt

1. Preheat the oven to 400 degrees.

2. In a food processor, add the self-rising flour, butter, and cheddar cheese.

3. Pulse until the butter and cheese are well incorporated into the flour.

4. Add the yogurt and pulse until it forms a ball.

5. Remove the dough from the food processor and add additional flour if needed to hold the dough together.

6. Roll the dough into 12 small balls using your well floured hands. Place the balls close together and bake until lightly browned and puffed. (I prefer to bake mine in a tin pie pan.) Serve immediately.

NOTE: For a little spice, add some cayenne pepper when you add the yogurt.

Gerry Austin's Irish Soda Bread

My editor, Michael Austin, got this recipe from his mother when he was in his late teens or early twenties, and he has been making it ever since. When we had our first meeting for this book he made a loaf for me and brought it to my house. I knew after one bite that it was the best Irish soda bread I had ever tasted.

6	cups all-purpose flour		1	(15-ounce) package dark raisins
1	cup sugar			
1	teaspoon baking soda		6	large eggs
1	teaspoon salt		3	cups buttermilk
			1	tablespoon vegetable oil

1. Preheat the oven to 350 degrees. Lightly grease two 9-inch round cake pans and set aside.

2. Combine the flour, sugar, soda, salt, and raisins in a large bowl.

3. In a separate bowl, combine the eggs, buttermilk, and oil, mixing until the eggs are broken.

4. Move the dry ingredients to the sides of the large bowl and pour the liquid ingredients into the center. Fold the dry ingredients over the liquid pool with your hands until the dough is sticky.

5. Scoop the dough from the bowl, dividing it between the prepared pans.

6. Bake for one hour. Test for doneness with a sharp knife, making the shape of a cross in the center of each loaf. If the knife comes out clean, the bread is done.

7. Serve warm with softened butter.

May there be a generation of children
On the children of your children.
—TRADITIONAL IRISH BLESSING

WHEN I WAS A LITTLE KID WE OFTEN HAD PIZZA
for Sunday supper. Sunday dinner (lunch) in the South usually was a
big fancy meal with a zillion types of vegetables, meats, breads, and
desserts, but supper was our favorite Sunday meal. My mother would
take store-bought pizzas and dress them up with her own fresh
vegetables, pepperoni, and extra cheese. Now, so many years later, I
still love great pizza. My backyard wood-burning brick oven can crank
out a lot of pizzas. This is a good thing, because my guests absolutely
adore them.

Easy Pizza Dough

MAKES 4 PIZZA SHELLS

Pizza is one of my favorite foods and brings back so many wonderful memories. Here is a simple recipe that makes a great crispy crust. Pizza dough is best when you allow it to rest overnight before you roll it out.

1 cup warm water, 95 to 115 degrees

2 teaspoons active dry yeast

2 teaspoons honey

¼ cup extra virgin olive oil

3½ cups all-purpose or multigrain flour

Pinch of kosher salt

1. In a food processor, combine the warm water, yeast, honey, and olive oil and mix well. Process until the yeast dissolves and the mixture is bubbly.

2. Add the flour and pulse. Add a pinch of salt and pulse again. Run the food processor until the dough makes a ball.

3. Remove and place on a lightly floured surface and knead for 2 minutes.

4. Place in a lightly greased bowl, cover well, and refrigerate overnight.

5. Remove the dough from the refrigerator and divide into 4 pieces. Roll into 4 small pizzas.

Basic Tomato Sauce

MAKES 2 CUPS SAUCE

This is a great sauce to keep in the refrigerator for pizza or any other wonderful Italian dish. I make this sauce using fresh tomatoes, then I preserve it in jars and store it so it will be ready to use in the winter.

¼ cup extra virgin olive oil

1 small onion, diced

6 cloves garlic, minced

½ teaspoon crushed red pepper flakes

1 tablespoon chopped fresh thyme

1 tablespoon brown sugar

12 ounces stewed tomatoes, diced or whole

1 tablespoon dried oregano or 2 tablespoons fresh

1 tablespoon chopped fresh rosemary

¼ cup chopped fresh basil

Salt and freshly ground black pepper to taste

1. Heat the olive oil in a medium saucepan over medium-low heat. When hot, add the onion and slowly sauté while stirring, 6 to 8 minutes.

2. Add the garlic, red pepper flakes, and thyme and cook for another 6 minutes. In this recipe we are not looking for color; rather, we are slowly releasing the flavors of the ingredients by cooking them at a low temperature.

3. Add the brown sugar and stir until it is dissolved, then add the stewed tomatoes.

4. Bring the sauce to a low simmer. Be sure to stir often enough so that the bottom does not scorch. Cook for 20 minutes.

5. Finally, add the remaining fresh herbs and cook for 6 to 8 minutes more, adding salt and pepper to taste. If the sauce is too rustic for your taste, puree in a blender until it reaches the desired consistency.

Caramelized Onions

Makes 2 cups

Every kitchen should stock this wonderful topping. I love to make mine using sweet Vidalia onions when they are in season.

2	tablespoons unsalted butter	3	tablespoons balsamic vinegar
2	tablespoons olive oil		Salt and freshly ground black pepper to taste
4	onions, cut in half and thinly sliced		

1. Heat butter and olive oil in a medium saucepan over medium low.

2. When the butter is melted, add the onions. If it looks overfilled, don't worry— they are going to cook down, and you will wish you had prepared more! Stir the onions, making sure that they are coated. Cook for 10 minutes.

3. When the onions begin to caramelize, add the balsamic vinegar.

4. Cook for another 20 minutes until soft and dark brown. Do not increase the heat to rush the color. These wonderfully sweet onions take time and require a little patience.

5. Season with salt and pepper and reserve for other dishes.

Roasted Apples

It might seem strange, but apples are great on pizza. They add a wonderful tartness and sweetness. This variety of pizza is perfect for a cool fall night.

3   apples, unpeeled and thinly sliced

2   tablespoons unsalted butter, melted

2   tablespoons brown sugar

1   teaspoon honey

Pinch of salt

1. Preheat the oven to 325 degrees.

2. In a large bowl, toss all the ingredients, making sure the apples are well coated.

3. Lightly grease a half sheet pan lined with parchment paper. Lay out the apple slices in a single layer to cook evenly.

4. Place in the oven for 10 minutes. Remove and rotate. Return to the oven for 3 to 5 more minutes and then remove to cool on a wire rack.

5. Set aside for other dishes—pizza, soups, salads, desserts, and for garnish.

Margherita Pizza

MAKES 1 (8 OR 9-INCH) PIZZA

This is the classic Neapolitan pizza created for Queen Margherita of Italy. It is topped with simply tomatoes, basil and mozzarella cheese.

1	recipe Easy Pizza Dough (see page 256)	2	thin slices prosciutto
3	tablespoons homemade marinara sauce	½	cup chopped arugula
4	slices dry mozzarella		Freshly ground black pepper to taste
4	leaves fresh basil, chopped		

1. Preheat the oven to 400 degrees with a pizza stone in the oven.

2. Prepare the pizza dough according to the recipe. Divide the pizza dough into fourths. Roll out one of the pieces to 8 or 9 inches in diameter. Place the dough on a lightly floured pizza peel, or baking sheet with no sides, and top with the sauce, cheese, and basil.

3. Slide the unbaked pizza onto the hot stone and bake until the crust is brown and bubbly, about 20 minutes.

4. Remove from the oven and top with the prosciutto, arugula, and pepper. Slice and serve immediately.

NOTE: Tightly wrap the remaining three pieces of pizza dough in plastic wrap and store in the refrigerator or freezer for future use.

Pizza with Roasted Apples
and Chicken Livers

MAKES 1 (8 OR 9-INCH) PIZZA

Okay, pizza with chicken livers? Yes, it is amazing! We first made it with foie gras, *but lightly sautéed chicken livers chopped up and added to the pizza make for some great eating, too. I also love the sweetness of the apples and caramelized onions.*

1	Easy Pizza Dough recipe (see recipe on page 256)
4	chicken livers, cleaned and sautéed
	Roasted apples (see recipe on page 259)
¼	cup caramelized onions (see recipe on page 258)
4	to 6 ounces fresh arugula
3	tablespoons apple cider reduction (see pantry)
	Truffle oil
	Salt and freshly ground black pepper to taste

1. Preheat the oven to 400 degrees with a pizza stone in the oven.

2. Prepare the pizza dough according to the recipe. Divide the pizza dough into fourths. Roll out one of the pieces to 8 or 9 inches in diameter. Place the dough on a lightly floured pizza peel, or baking sheet with no sides.

3. Top the dough with the chicken livers, apples, and onions. Slide the unbaked pizza onto the hot stone. Bake for 20 to 25 minutes.

4. When the pizza dough has a nice crust, remove and place the arugula on top.

5. Drizzle with the cider reduction and oil, then season with salt and pepper. Cut into four pieces and serve immediately.

NOTE: Tightly wrap the remaining three pieces of pizza dough in plastic wrap and store in the refrigerator or freezer for future use.

Pizza with Goat Cheese and Arugula

MAKES 1 (8 OR 9-INCH) PIZZA

There is nothing better than a crunchy pizza crust slathered with goat cheese and herbs. When you add the arugula it makes the pizza almost like a great sandwich.

1   Easy Pizza Dough recipe (see recipe on page 256)

¼   cup caramelized onions (see recipe on page 258)

3   sprigs fresh rosemary

1   tablespoon chopped fresh thyme

4   to 6 ounces goat cheese, crumbled

4   to 6 ounces arugula

    Olive oil for drizzling

    Salt and freshly ground black pepper to taste

1. Preheat the oven to 400 degrees with a pizza stone in the oven.

2. Prepare the pizza dough according to the recipe. Divide the pizza dough into fourths. Roll out one of the pieces to 8 or 9 inches in diameter. Place the dough on a lightly floured pizza peel, or baking sheet with no sides.

3. Top the dough with the onions, rosemary, thyme, and crumbled goat cheese. Bake on the hot stone for 20 to 25 minutes.

4. When the dough has a nice crust, remove it from the oven and place the mache on top.

5. Drizzle with the olive oil and season with salt and pepper. Cut into four pieces and serve immediately.

NOTE: Tightly wrap the remaining three pieces of pizza dough in plastic wrap and store in the refrigerator or freezer for future use.

Pizza with Prosciutto and Olives

MAKES 1 (8 OR 9-INCH) PIZZA

This is a pizza that is hard not to love: a crispy crust topped with slices of good prosciutto, spinach, olives, and one of my favorite cheeses, Manchego from Spain. I add the prosciutto after baking because the ham can become saltier when it is heated.

1	Easy Pizza Dough recipe (see recipe on page 256)	¼	cup fresh spinach
2	tablespoons pitted and sliced black or green olives	12	slices prosciutto
¼	cup shredded manchego cheese		Olive oil for drizzling
			Freshly ground black pepper to taste

1. Preheat the oven to 400 degrees with a pizza stone in the oven.

2. Prepare the pizza dough according to the recipe. Divide the pizza dough into fourths. Roll out one of the pieces to 8 or 9 inches in diameter. Place the dough on a lightly floured pizza peel, or baking sheet with no sides.

3. Top the dough with the olives and manchego cheese. Bake on the hot stone for 20 to 25 minutes, checking periodically.

4. When the dough has a nice crust, remove it from the oven and place the spinach on top.

5. Top with the prosciutto, then drizzle with oil and season with pepper. Cut into four pieces and serve immediately.

NOTE: Tightly wrap the remaining three pieces of pizza dough in plastic wrap and store in the refrigerator or freezer for future use.

Pizza with Quail Eggs and Bacon

MAKES 1 (8 OR 9-INCH) PIZZA

I love the delicate taste of quail eggs. Here in the Midwest, apple-smoked bacon is fantastic. This variation makes a great breakfast pizza.

1	Easy Pizza Dough recipe (see recipe on page 256)	¼	cup shredded white cheddar cheese
6	strips apple-wood smoked bacon, chopped	6	quail eggs
			Olive oil for drizzling
2	tablespoons minced fresh chives		

1. Preheat the oven to 400 degrees with a pizza stone in the oven.

2. Prepare the pizza dough according to the recipe. Divide the pizza dough into fourths. Roll out one of the pieces to 8 or 9 inches in diameter. Place the dough on a lightly floured pizza peel, or baking sheet with no sides.

3. Top the dough with the bacon, chives, and shredded cheese. Gently crack 3 quail eggs per pizza on top.

4. Carefully transfer to the oven and bake on the hot stone for 20 to 25 minutes, checking periodically.

5. When the dough has a nice crust, remove it from the oven and place the spinach on top. Drizzle with olive oil. Cut into four pieces and serve immediately.

NOTE: Tightly wrap the remaining three pieces of pizza dough in plastic wrap and store in the refrigerator or freezer for future use.

May the saddest day of your future be no worse
Than the happiest day of your past.
—TRADITIONAL IRISH BLESSING

TRAINING WITH THREE FRENCH CHEFS TAUGHT

me the secret to a great meal—the sauce. My beloved Julia Child never steered me wrong with one of her great sauces. Pierre Glardone and Albert Ughetto taught me fine French sauces, as well. As I traveled more I learned that sauces were universal, not just the domain of the French. My dear chef Rey Villalobos makes the best salsa ever. His salsa de arbor and salsa verde are little pots of tastes and fire that will rock your meal. I also love sweet sauces, such as our chocolate tequila sauce with fresh fruit, or a great piece of cake.

Is it really a meal if it does not include a dessert? Hard to say. Dessert is that end-of-the-meal rainbow. You've been good and eaten all of your vegetables and now you are ready for your prize. As a child I loved dessert, and we always got more of it after Sunday dinners. There is nothing better than my aunt Evelyn's pound cake with fresh strawberries. And speaking of my childhood desserts, who could resist a slice of ice box pie? A little bit of sweetness is good for us. I hope you enjoy our dessert recipes. And remember, life is about living, and living fully. And yes, you can have your cake and eat it, too. As long as you have it in moderation.

Salsa de Chile de Arbol

MAKES 1 QUART

My chef Rey Villalobos makes this salsa with these small, dry chiles, which impart a nice flavor and heat. All I can say about this recipe is WOW!

10 to 15 dried chiles de arbol

1 (12-ounce) can diced tomatoes with juice

1½ cloves garlic

Salt and freshly ground black pepper to taste

1. Place a large sauté pan over high heat. When hot, place the dried chiles in the pan.

2. Toast for 2 to 3 minutes while tossing.

3. Remove from the heat. When cool enough to handle, remove and discard the top stems.

4. Put the chiles, tomatoes, and garlic into a blender and pulse 5 to 6 times. Season with salt and pepper. Serve immediately or refrigerate for later use.

Salsa Verde

MAKES 1 QUART

Made fresh, this salsa holds up for two days. You can half the recipe, but it probably will be gone too quickly. Use it from breakfast and eggs to pork and vegetables. This makes everything fabulous!

1	head iceberg lettuce	¼	cup water
1	to 2 jalapeño peppers, depending on taste	2	limes, juiced
2	cloves garlic		Salt and freshly ground black pepper to taste
1	cup fresh cilantro		

1. Place the green parts of the lettuce leaves into a blender. Try not to use the white bitter part of the lettuce.

2. Add the peppers, garlic, cilantro, and water to the blender.

3. Blend well. You may have to push the ingredients down in order for the blades to catch. Add the lime juice and season with salt and pepper.

Chocolate Tequila Sauce

MAKES 2¹/₂ CUPS SAUCE

I serve this wonderful chocolate sauce with mango soufflé. It's a very easy dessert sauce that can be made in advance, kept in the refrigerator, and reheated when needed. I invented this sauce for my friend Jeffrey Hopmeyer, creator of the beautiful El Diamante del Cielo Tequila.

2	cups chopped semisweet chocolate	¹/₄	cup tequila
		1	cup heavy cream

1. Combine the chocolate, tequila, and cream in a saucepan over medium-low heat.

2. Heat, stirring occasionally, until the chocolate is melted and the sauce begins to combine nicely.

NOTE: Great with fresh fruit or soufflés!

Strawberry Sauce

This is my favorite sauce to put into my yogurt egg-white soufflés. (See Strawberry Soufflé recipe on page 283.) It is incredibly simple, and great on its own, too. It is best with fresh strawberries, but if necessary, you can use frozen ones.

1	pint (2 cups) fresh strawberries, capped and cut in quarters	3	tablespoons sugar
		2	tablespoons water

1. Place the strawberries, sugar, and water in a medium saucepan over medium-high heat.

2. Bring to a boil for 1 minute, then reduce the heat and simmer slowly while stirring constantly.

3. When the mixture has thickened and reached syrup consistency, remove from the heat and cool.

4. When cool, place into a blender and puree until smooth.

Crème Anglais with Orange Zest

What is dessert without this superb sauce? It takes practice to make it velvety, but once you've made it a couple of times, you will always keep some in your fridge. If you want to cheat, just melt a little bit of vanilla ice cream—that's not too bad either. You can also chill this sauce, put it in an ice cream machine, and make wonderful homemade ice cream.

2	egg yolks	1	tablespoon freshly squeezed orange juice
½	cup sugar		
½	cup heavy cream	1	teaspoon orange zest

1. Whisk the egg yolks and the sugar in a small saucepan over low heat. Do not stop whisking until the mixture begins to thicken, about 2 minutes.

2. Add the heavy cream and juice. Continue to whisk until the sauce begins to thicken again, another 2 minutes. Remove from the heat when the consistency resembles pudding.

3. Add the orange zest and continue to whisk until thoroughly combined.

4. When cool, cover and refrigerate. This will keep for up to two days.

Sonja's Cinnamon Rolls

These delightful sweet rolls are a staple at Sonja's Restaurant in Missouri. They have a secret ingredient in them—instant pudding. You can use instant or make your own vanilla pudding. I have tried both, and for some strange reason the instant pudding rolls come out better. You can also add chocolate pudding and make a chocolate frosting, which is fantastic. All I can say is, these rolls are really good no matter which way you decide to go.

Dough

1 (14-ounce) can sweetened condensed milk

4 egg yolks

2 tablespoons butter

1 tablespoon cornstarch

1 (3½-ounce) box instant vanilla pudding

2 eggs, beaten

½ cup (1 stick) unsalted butter, melted

½ cup warm water, 100 to 110 degrees

2 tablespoons sugar

2 (¼-ounce) packages active dry yeast

6 cups bread flour, sifted

Filling

2 cups brown sugar

4 teaspoons ground cinnamon

Frosting

1 (8-ounce) package cream cheese, softened

1 cup (2 sticks) butter, softened

8 ounces (½ box) powdered sugar

Milk

1. **For the dough,** place the sweetened condensed milk, egg yolks, 2 tablespoons butter, and cornstarch in the top of a double boiler over medium heat. Stir constantly and cook until custard coats the back of a spoon.

2. Remove from the heat and chill in the refrigerator for 20 minutes.

3. Meanwhile, in a large bowl, make the pudding according to directions on the box, then stir in 2 beaten eggs and the melted butter.

4. Combine the pudding with the chilled custard mixture, stirring well. Set aside.

5. Add the sugar and yeast to warm water, stirring well to combine. Let stand 10 minutes.

6. Add the yeast mixture to the pudding mixture, then stir in the sifted bread flour, 1 cup at a time. You can also complete this step with a stand mixer, adding 1 cup of flour at a time. The dough will make a soft ball.

7. Transfer the dough to a well-oiled bowl, cover, and refrigerate overnight.

8. **For the filling,** combine the sugar and cinnamon in small bowl and set aside.

9. **To make the rolls,** remove the dough from the refrigerator and on a lightly floured surface roll to slightly flatten. Allow it to double in bulk, about 2 hours.

10. After the dough has doubled, divide it in half and roll each half into a large 8 x 12-inch piece, then sprinkle with half of the filling mixture.

11. Roll each one jelly-roll–style and slice with a serrated knife.

12. Place the rolls on a heavily greased sheet pan. Do not crowd them. Give the rolls enough room to double in bulk once more. Place a light cloth over them.

13. Preheat the oven to 350 degrees.

14. When the rolls have doubled in bulk, remove the cloth and bake for 25 minutes or until light brown.

15. Meanwhile **make the frosting** by creaming the butter and cream cheese in the bowl of an electric mixer on medium speed. Reduce the speed and add the powdered sugar. Use milk to thin if the frosting is too thick.

16. Remove the rolls from the oven and cool slightly on a wire rack. Spread with the cream cheese frosting and serve warm.

Ice Box Pie

My life as a chef has provided me the opportunity to meet many other great chefs. One of them is Wilbert Jones, who has been in my life for many years. He created this fabulous recipe. Genius!

As the name suggests, typical ice box pies are not baked. Egg whites are used in this recipe, however, so thirty minutes of baking time is required. Afterward the pie is chilled in the refrigerator, and then served cold.

Shell

1¼ cups all-purpose flour

¼ teaspoon salt

¼ cup vegetable shortening

2 tablespoons unsalted butter

2 tablespoons ice water, or as needed

Filling

6 egg whites

1 cup sugar

2 teaspoons pure vanilla extract

1 cup graham crackers

1 cup chopped pecans

1½ cups sweetened coconut flakes

½ teaspoon ground cinnamon

1. **For the pie shell,** place all of the ingredients in a medium mixing bowl and mix on low speed with an electric mixer until lightly blended.

2. Gently use your hands to form the dough into a ball.

3. Roll out between sheets of waxed paper into a 10-inch circle.

4. Remove the waxed paper and place the dough in a 9-inch pie pan.

5. Press the dough against the pan firmly, and trim away any extra dough.

6. For a decorative edge, press the rim with a fork. Makes one 9-inch pie shell.

7. Preheat the oven to 350 degrees.

8. **For the pie filling,** place the egg whites in a medium mixing bowl and beat with an electric mixer on high until stiff peaks are formed. Fold in the remaining ingredients.

9. Pour the mixture into the pie shell.

10. Bake for 30 minutes or until a knife inserted in the middle comes out clean.

11. Cool to room temperature, then cover and chill in the refrigerator until you are ready to serve.

Rum Raisin Sweet Potato Pie

MAKES 8 SERVINGS

I love my friend chef Wilbert Jones's light southern food, and I have enjoyed many meals at his home. Here is a wonderful pie he brought to a holiday dinner.

1	cup sugar	½	teaspoon vanilla bean seeds
½	teaspoon ground nutmeg	½	cup buttermilk
½	teaspoon ground cinnamon	1	cup dark raisins, soaked 2 hours in ¼ cup dark rum
2	cups cooked and mashed sweet potatoes	1	Pie shell recipe (see recipe on page 278)
1	egg		
1	tablespoon orange zest		

1. Preheat the oven to 425 degrees.

2. Combine all the ingredients except the raisins and rum in a large mixing bowl.

3. Mix on medium speed with an electric mixer until the texture is smooth.

4. Fold in the raisins and rum, then pour into a pie shell and bake for 10 minutes.

5. Reduce the temperature to 350 degrees. Bake for an additional 45 minutes or until the filling is set or a knife inserted into the center comes out clean. Cool on a wire rack.

Banana-Blueberry Muffin Tops

Breakfast is one of my favorite meals, but sometimes I don't feel like eating a big breakfast, so I make these for my houseguests. My sister-in-law, Andrea, loves these for breakfast served with one of my famous cafe lattes.

1 cup self-rising flour, sifted	¼ cup non-fat milk
1 cup breakfast cereal, soaked in non-fat milk	1 egg, slightly beaten
½ cup mashed bananas	4 tablespoons safflower oil
⅓ cup sugar	½ cup fresh blueberries

1. Preheat the oven to 400 degrees.

2. Thoroughly grease a muffin-top pan.

3. Put the self-rising flour in a large bowl. In another bowl, combine the soaked breakfast cereal, bananas, sugar, milk, egg, and safflower oil and beat well.

4. Carefully mix the wet ingredients into the flour, then carefully fold in the blueberries.

5. Spoon the batter into the muffin pan and bake 12 to 15 minutes, or until a toothpick inserted in the center comes out clean. Serve warm with white cheddar cheese and jam.

Bread Pudding

MAKES 8 SERVINGS

This is one of the oldest and best desserts. It may sound crazy, but it simply does not taste great unless the bread is stale. I love using brioche, which was not a part of my world until I worked as a fancy chef in the North. Back home in Jasper, Grandmother Georgia made her bread pudding out of Pullman loaf, a humble white bread. I think this recipe came from the old days at her boarding house for railroad employees.

1	loaf brioche, cut into medium-size cubes	1	cup heavy cream
1½	cups sugar	½	cup half-and-half
2	teaspoons pure vanilla extract	1	cup golden raisins
10	eggs	½	cup toasted chopped pecans

1. Preheat the oven to 350 degrees.

2. Spread the brioche cubes evenly in a lightly greased 13 x 9-inch casserole dish.

3. Place all the remaining ingredients into a large bowl and combine.

4. Pour the mixture over the bread and let sit for 10 minutes.

5. Bake for 35 to 40 minutes or until a knife inserted in the center comes out clean. I love a golden brown color on top.

6. Serve hot or cold. This bread pudding is absolutely delicious with ice cream.

Strawberry Soufflé

MAKES 4 SERVINGS

My dear friend Jeffrey Pollak gave me this recipe. It originally came from a famous Chicago restaurant, Le Peroqua. This wonderful yogurt and egg–white soufflé is so special that no one will believe it is not as fattening as other soufflés. I make this soufflé time and time again for special dinners. Thank you, Jeffrey, for sharing this great recipe. Here's to many great soufflés in your family's food life!

	Butter	1	recipe Strawberry Sauce (see recipe on page 274)
	Sugar		
4	egg whites	8	ounces strawberry yogurt
½	cup sugar		Your favorite chocolate sauce

1. Preheat the oven to 375 degrees.

2. Coat 4 ramekins with butter and sugar.

3. Whip the egg whites on high speed of an electric mixer while gradually adding the sugar. Beat until stiff peaks form.

4. Fold in the strawberry sauce and yogurt.

5. Fill the ramekins and place in a baking dish. Pour enough water into the baking dish to come 1 inch up the sides of the ramkins.

6. Bake for 8 to 10 minutes or until the tops are lightly browned and spring back to the touch.

7. Top with chocolate sauce and serve immediately.

Flan

Chef Rey makes the most perfect flan. Here is the recipe for his beautifully silky custard, which has been a staple of many of his family's parties.

4	tablespoons sugar	2	(14-ounce) cans sweetened condensed milk
3	large eggs		
2	tablespoons pure vanilla extract	1	(12-ounce) can evaporated milk

1. Preheat the oven to 350 degrees. Bring a medium-size pot of water to a slow simmer.

2. Place the sugar in a small stainless steel bowl. Hold the bowl with a glove or towel over medium heat. Rotate the bowl until the sugar begins to melt and caramelize, coating as much of the bowl as possible.

3. When the sugar has melted, place the bowl in the freezer for 10 minutes to harden.

4. Combine the eggs, vanilla, and both milks in a mixing bowl and beat with an electric mixer for 2 to 3 minutes.

5. Remove the bowl from the freezer and pour the egg mixture into the caramel-coated bowl.

6. Cover tightly with foil and place in a baking dish. Fill the baking dish with the reserved simmering water halfway up the sides. Carefully place in the oven and bake for 1 hour.

7. Gently remove from the oven. Remove the foil and pierce the center of the flan with a knife. The knife should come out clean. If not, place the flan back into the hot water bath, cover, and cook for another 30 minutes. Cool to room temperature, then place in the refrigerator for 1 to 2 hours to chill.

8. To remove from the mold, place the bowl over low heat for 10 seconds and flip the bowl onto a plate. Serve.

Caramelized Bananas

MAKES 4 SERVINGS

This dish is made with tiny Cuban finger bananas, which can be sweeter and starchier than regular bananas. I love this dish served on a buffet along with other desserts.

2	tablespoons unsalted butter	2	tablespoons sugar
4	cups finger bananas or two large bananas, peeled and sliced	½	teaspoon ground cinnamon
		1	tablespoon tequila

1. Heat the butter in a large sauté pan over medium-high heat until it sizzles.

2. Add the bananas and allow them to brown on each side. Add the sugar, cinnamon, and tequila. Be careful when adding the tequila, because the heat can ignite the liquor.

3. Shake the pan until the liquid thickens.

4. Serve with ice cream and caramel sauce.

Black Walnut Cake

This is my mother's recipe. She made this for our big family gatherings, and I have always loved it. You must use black walnuts, which are available in season at the market.

½ cup butter, softened

½ cup vegetable shortening

2 cups sugar

5 large eggs, separated

1 cup buttermilk

1 teaspoon baking soda

2 cups all-purpose flour

1 teaspoon pure vanilla extract

1 cup chopped black walnuts

¼ cup flaked coconut

½ teaspoon cream of tartar

3 tablespoons light rum

Cream Cheese Frosting (see recipe on page 287)

Walnut halves for garnish

1. Preheat the oven to 350 degrees.

2. Grease three 9-inch round cake pans and dust them well with flour. Or line the bottoms of the pans with waxed paper, then grease the waxed paper and dust with flour. Set the pans aside.

3. Beat the butter and shortening until creamy. Gradually add the sugar, beating well.

4. Add the egg yolks one at a time to the mixture, beating well after each addition.

5. In a small bowl, combine the buttermilk and baking soda and stir until the soda is dissolved.

6. With your mixer on low, add some flour to the butter mixture, add the buttermilk mixture, then add the rest of the flour.

7. Stir in the vanilla, walnuts, and coconut.

8. In another bowl, beat the egg whites on high speed until foamy, then add the cream of tartar and beat until stiff peaks form.

9. Gently fold the stiff egg whites into the cake batter and pour into the prepared pans.

10. Bake 20 to 25 minutes or until a cake tester comes out clean. Remove from the oven and cool 5 minutes in the pans. Remove from the pans, brush rum on the tops of the layers, and finish cooling on wire racks.

11. When completely cool, stack the cakes and spread with the cream cheese frosting over the stacked cake. Garnish with walnut halves.

Cream Cheese Frosting

MAKES ABOUT 3 CUPS

¾ cup (1½ sticks) butter, softened

1 (8-ounce) package cream cheese, softened

1 pound sifted powdered sugar

1 teaspoon pure vanilla extract

1. Using a mixer, completely whip the softened butter and cream cheese.

2. Reduce the mixer speed and slowly incorporate the powdered sugar, then add the vanilla. Spread on cooled layers.

Sarah's Chocolate Birthday Cake

MAKES TWO 9-INCH CAKES OR 40 CUPCAKES

My beloved Sarah made this chocolate cake for my forty-sixth birthday. Everyone just adored it. She is the queen of fine pastries and candies on Chicago's famed Oak Street.

Chocolate Cake

1 cup cocoa powder

3 ⅓ cups boiling water

3 ⅓ cups cake flour

4 ⅓ cups sugar

4 tablespoons plus ½ teaspoon baking powder

2 ½ teaspoons salt

10 eggs

2 tablespoons plus ½ teaspoon vanilla extract

2 ½ cups unsalted butter

1. Preheat the oven to 350 degrees.

2. Combine the cocoa powder and boiling water and let cool.

3. Combine the flour, sugar, baking powder, and salt and stir for 30 seconds to mix well.

4. Combine one-third of the cocoa mixture with the eggs.

5. Add the remaining cocoa mixture and butter to the dry ingredients and mix for 1 ½ minutes.

6. Add the cocoa and egg mixture to the cocoa and flour mixture in three batches and stir for 20 seconds between each addition, scraping the sides of the bowl.

7. Pour the batter into two 9-inch pans lined with parchment paper and brushed with butter and flour.

8. Bake for about 35 minutes, or until a toothpick inserted into the center of the cake comes out clean.

Chocolate Buttercream

Makes enough to frost two 9-inch cakes

8	egg whites		½	cup water
	Pinch of salt		6	cups unsalted butter, softened
2¾ cups sugar			4	cups (16½ ounces) chocolate, melted

1. Combine the egg whites and salt in the work bowl of a stand mixer. Set the mixer to whisk on low.

2. Combine the sugar and water in a heavy pot on medium heat and cook until it reaches 118 degrees.

3. Turn the mixer on high and careful pour the sugar syrup into the lightly beaten egg whites. Turn the speed to medium and allow to cool slightly.

4. Add the soften butter 1 cup at a time, whisking on low after each addition.

5. Add the melted chocolate and whisk to combine. (You can use any bittersweet chocolate you like or even milk chocolate.) Keep at room temperature until ready to ice the cakes.

Rena Jones Thornton's Red Velvet Cake

MAKES 12 SERVINGS

My cousin Rena makes this, and it is the best red velvet cake I have ever tasted. Rena sometimes makes large cakes, and usually big cakes don't taste so great, but somehow Rena's always do. I wish every wedding cake would taste this good.

3	extra large eggs	1	cup buttermilk
2	cups sugar	1	tablespoon butter flavoring
1	to 2 ounces red food coloring	1/2	teaspoon plus a pinch of baking soda
2	tablespoons cocoa	1 1/4	tablespoons white vinegar
1	cup (2 sticks) butter, softened		Cream Cheese Frosting (see recipe on page 287)
2 1/2	cups sifted cake flour		
1 1/4	teaspoons salt		

1. Preheat the oven to 350 degrees. Grease and flour two 9-inch cake pans. Set aside.

2. With an electric mixer on medium speed, beat the eggs and sugar together until well combined.

3. Add the food coloring and cocoa, mixing well. Add the butter and mix well.

4. In a separate bowl, sift the flour and salt. Slowly add to the creamed mixture. Add the buttermilk and butter flavoring, mixing well.

5. In a small bowl, combine the vinegar and baking soda, stirring until the soda dissolves. Add to the creamed mixture.

6. Pour the batter into the prepared pans and bake about 20 minutes or until the cakes spring to the touch of the finger. You can make more layers by slicing the cakes horizontally, making them even thinner. Let the layers cool completely on wire racks before icing with Cream Cheese Frosting.

Aunt Evelyn's Pound Cake

I brought this dense, moist pound cake all the way from Florida to Chicago in a cooler. When I served it in my kitchen to my friends and family, they couldn't get enough of it. It was eaten in less time than it took me to drive it to Chicago—seventeen hours. My favorite way to enjoy this cake is sliced and served with assorted berries and whip cream. (See the photo on page 268.)

½	cup shortening	3	cups all-purpose flour
1	cup (2 sticks) butter, softened	½	teaspoon baking powder
3	cups sugar	1	cup milk
6	eggs	½	teaspoon pure vanilla extract

1. Preheat the oven to 325 degrees. Grease a large tube or angel food cake pan and set aside.

2. With an electric mixer on medium speed, cream together the shortening and butter while gradually adding the sugar.

3. Add the eggs, one at a time, beating well after each addition.

4. In a separate bowl, combine the flour and baking powder. Slowly add to the creamed mixture, then add the milk.

5. Add the vanilla. Beat well, about 5 minutes. Pour into the prepared pan.

6. Bake for 60 to 90 minutes, or until a cake tester inserted in the center comes out clean.

7. Remove from the oven, allow to cool for 6 to 7 minutes, and then invert the pan on a wire rack to cool for 1 hour. Carefully cut around the sides of the cake to remove.

Strawberry Pretzel Surprise

MAKES 16 SERVINGS

I got this recipe from my dear Aunt Evelyn. It is really easy to make, and perfect for a summer picnic.

Crust

2 cups crushed pretzels

6 tablespoons unsalted butter, melted

3 tablespoons sugar

Filling and Topping

1 (8-ounce) package cream cheese

1 cup sugar

1 (10-ounce) container frozen whipped topping, thawed

2 (3-ounce) packages strawberry-flavored gelatin

2 cups boiling water

1 (16-ounce) package frozen strawberries, thawed

1. **For the crust,** preheat the oven to 350 degrees. Lightly grease a 13 x 9-inch baking dish and set aside.

2. In a medium bowl, combine the pretzels, butter, and sugar.

3. Pat the pretzel mixture into the bottom of the prepared dish.

4. Bake for 10 minutes. Cool completely on a wire rack and set aside.

5. **For the filling and topping,** in a large bowl, beat the cream cheese and sugar until smooth.

6. Fold in the whipped topping and spread over the cooled crust. Set aside.

7. In another bowl, dissolve the gelatin in the boiling water. Add the strawberries.

8. Place the bowl over a larger bowl of ice water and refrigerate, stirring occasionally, until the mixture starts to thicken slightly.

9. Spoon the strawberry mixture over the cream cheese mixture.

10. Cover and refrigerate for 4 hours. Cut into 16 squares and serve cold.

German Chocolate Cake

Here is a truly decadent dessert that always pleases chocolate lovers.

4	(1-ounce) squares German sweet chocolate	2	cups sugar
2	cups all-purpose flour	4	eggs, separated
1	teaspoon baking soda	1	teaspoon pure vanilla extract
¼	teaspoon salt	1	cup buttermilk
1	cup (2 sticks) butter	1	recipe Pecan-Coconut Frosting (see recipe on page 295)

1. Preheat the oven to 350 degrees.

2. Grease the sides of three 8- or 9-inch cake pans, and line the bottoms with waxed paper. Set aside.

3. Melt the chocolate in the top of a double boiler over low heat, stirring constantly, about 4 minutes. Or place the chocolate in a glass bowl and microwave on high for 1 to 2 minutes. Stir well after each minute. Set aside.

4. In a medium bowl, combine the flour, baking soda, and salt and set aside.

5. In a large mixing bowl, with an electric mixer beat the butter and sugar on medium speed until light and fluffy. Add the egg yolks, one at a time, beating well after each addition.

6. Fold in the melted chocolate and the vanilla.

7. Add the flour mixture and the buttermilk and blend well.

8. Beat the egg whites in another large bowl with an electric mixer on high speed until stiff peaks form. Gently fold into the batter.

9. Pour evenly into prepared pans.

10. Bake in a 350 degree oven for 30 minutes or until a cake tester inserted into the center comes out clean.

11. Cool for 15 minutes before removing the cakes from the pans. Remove the waxed paper, then cool the cakes completely on wire racks before spreading with Pecan-Coconut Frosting.

Pecan-Coconut Frosting

2   (12-ounce) cans evaporated milk
3   cups sugar
1½ cups (3 sticks) butter, softened
8   egg yolks, slightly beaten
3   teaspoons pure vanilla extract
1   (14-ounce) package flaked coconut
3   cups chopped pecans

1. Combine the milk, sugar, butter, egg yolks, and vanilla in a large saucepan and cook over medium heat for 12 to 15 minutes, stirring constantly until thick and golden brown.

2. Remove from the heat. Add the coconut and pecans. Mix well.

3. Cool to room temperature. Makes enough to fill and frost the top and sides of a three-layer cake.

CHAPTER 8

Returning Back to the Family

The place I was born is tucked away in a lush and wooded pocket of northern Florida. It is a remote place heavy with towering pine trees, and thus, a place well known to Southerners at one time for its abundance of turpentine stills. People always think of beaches, palm trees, and lawn flamingos when they think of Florida, but my corner of the Sunshine State was a very rural, very southern place. My charming hometown became easily accessible to the rest of the country only when Highway 41 was built, and later, Interstate 75. Motorists knew it as the first little town you saw when you crossed the Georgia-Florida state line. Once dotted with boarding houses and neon signs welcoming motorists to little pink retro motels, this was my home. And let me tell you, some very fine cooking graced those roadside oases.

Growing up in northern Florida, everything centered around the farm, where my family has tended the land for more than one hundred years, planting tobacco, corn, soybeans, and later raising cattle. This closeness to the earth taught me so much about life and my passion for food. Like most children I didn't appreciate that little window of time in my life, but as I've grown older I sometimes wish I could just be transported back.

Even the seasons form a great circle in their changing, and always come back again to where they were. The life of a man is a circle from childhood to childhood, and so it is in everything where power moves.

—BLACK ELK (OGLALA) 1863–1950

As a child, I dreamed of moving to the big city to realize my dreams. Trips to my grandmother Mabel's in Miami helped to satisfy that early need to see the world outside of Jasper, and being introduced to a different culture was important to my development. My beloved Aunt Opason, or "Mary," was of Japanese heritage and taught me about Asian culture through food. These wonderful lessons not only taught me the importance of diversity, but also expanded my palate, which fueled my passion for learning more and more about the world. I learned that being different was good. I learned that there was a great big world full of people just like me.

> This closeness to the earth taught me so much about life and my passion for food. Like most children I didn't appreciate that little window of time in my life, but as I've grown older I sometimes wish I could just be transported back.
>
> —ART

I knew if I stayed in Jasper I would become a farmer or the musical director of a Baptist church. My grandparents were hoping the latter would come true, but my love for dancing and my appreciation of a good gin and tonic blew that church dream away. I was lucky—I somehow learned to live not by what others dictated, but by what I felt in my heart was right for me. I learned that God is with us wherever we go and that He has a plan. The most important thing for me was to believe in myself and have faith that I could make my dreams come true.

Believe me, I went through great pain to get to where I am today. I suffered through many personal battles of self-doubt and discouragement, sometimes losing sight of the big picture. To escape my unhappiness in my younger years I would daydream or read books. Later I found relief in music and cooking. School was difficult for me, but I excelled in the classes that allowed me to dream and be creative.

My "Steel Magnolias"

Although it took some time for the men in my family to see the grand scheme of things, my mother and grandmothers were always understanding and patient with me, aware of my heart's desires. These women were fine southern ladies, real life "steel magnolias" who would feed anyone who came their way and who showed genuine kindness to strangers. But come between them and their children and prepare to feel a shoe against your head!

These beautiful women have truly inspired me to be the best I can be. One great woman I will celebrate and honor forever is Leila Curry. We all have people who come into our lives and bring us love, and sometimes they leave us as quickly as they arrived. I will never forget sitting on our screened-in porch shelling peas and listening to Leila's stories. She would sing gospel songs to me and shuffle her feet on the wooden floor. Her egg salad sandwiches were delightful, and she made the most amazing fried chicken.

When my grandmother died, and our farm was in danger of being sold by her heirs, my mother went into action to help our family keep the land we loved so much. She made sacrifices, including going to work full time when most women were home with their children. She did everything she could to help my father and to keep our family farm. I know it was hard for her but as Momma has continually told me from the earliest years, "God will take care of things." Well, God did take care of us, and Leila was sent to us as a "second mom."

I think of Leila as an earthbound angel, fulfilling some of the duties my mother couldn't perform while she was away at work. What would my life have been without sweet Leila? She taught me so much. I wish she could have stayed longer, but she was taken away. I can still recall the pain I felt when she died. When you lose someone so very close to you, it sometimes makes you numb. You lose the ability to feel for a while, and then you are faced with a choice: Do you become a victim of your tragedy, or do you use it to fuel your future vitality, and become a better, more complete person than you were? No one is immune to the cycle of life, but there are ways to cope. There are also ways to thrive.

I often wonder what my life would have been like without these women, and without having grown up in the tiny town of Jasper, Florida. I'm not really sure what made me want to explore. Had I chosen to stay put my life would have been worlds less complicated. Then again, the rewards of my hard work would not have been as great. My mother used to say to me, "You can always come back to the family," which for me was the sweetest notion. In my perfect scenario the family would come back to me, and join me in Chicago!

Jasper was a great place to grow up, but being a kid who was different from the rest made it tough. Little boys in Jasper drove tractors and worked on farms. I was a "Momma's boy" who wanted to play piano, perform on stage, and stay inside and cook. Mother, Leila, Grandmother Georgia, Grandmother Mabel, Aunt Brenda, and Aunt Evelyn were the great women who stood by me and defended me.

When it came time for me to leave Jasper, my mother cried. She still cries sometimes when I talk to her on the phone. But she knows it was all meant to be. When I was younger my mother was better than a therapist. Later I realized I needed to learn to cope with things myself, and not upset her with my worries, even though she was always eager to listen and hear what was on my mind. We talk daily, and my mother and father keep me posted on the latest, juiciest Jasper gossip. Sometimes I feel that life has taken me too far away.

Part of the reason I survived those early years away from Jasper was that my family sent me countless cakes and cookies to ease the pain of homesickness. As I said before, "Food is love," and it always has been. As I settle into my midforties, I am more appreciative and aware of what I left behind. Yes, I have countless friends who have become my new family in Chicago, but that little place I could not run fast enough to get away from is now calling me home.

> *Yes, I have countless friends who have become my new family in Chicago, but that little place I could not run fast enough to get away from is now calling me home.*
>
> —Art

The Twister and Grandmother's House

Recently a ferocious tornado, or "twister" as they're called in the South, destroyed my grandmother's home on our family farm. It was a simple shotgun-style house, long and narrow, and it stood under a cluster of century-old pecan trees that my great-grandfather planted. A freak storm took it all away from us in a matter of moments.

I have vivid memories of sitting on the porch at that house, the smell of gardenias thick in the steamy summer heat. I recall collecting the eggs that Daddy's prized chickens laid, and enjoying fresh goat's milk. We made the most wonderful peach ice cream, and with the pecans we picked up, we made amazing pecan pies. On homemade biscuits we drizzled freshly cooked cane syrup, and all around us there was love. What a life!

I want to rebuild that old house so that others can have the same wonderful life that I had. It's never the same when you go home. Everything looks smaller, and many of the people you knew have either moved away or passed on. But I need to go back and face the changes, even though it scares the living daylights out of me. As I grow older and hopefully wiser, I remind myself that everything is meant to be and that it will all work out. Maybe all the old familiar faces won't be there to greet me in Jasper, but something good will come out of my visit—I just know it.

Family Lessons and Passing Them On

When I was a boy, my great-aunt Millicent showed me the world. She also taught me that it was perfectly okay to like boiled peanuts and to enjoy eating acres of peas with boiled rice and sliced tomatoes in the summer. She blazed the trail for me, leaving home at a young age on her own journey of self-discovery. Returning home, she found that things had changed. She made the best of it, and now I must take that same love and those same lessons she so generously taught me and give them to my own nieces and great-nieces. God must know that our family needs wonderful women, because we sure have a lot of them!

I want to teach the children of my extended family what a vine-ripe tomato tastes like, and I want to teach them how to make a biscuit that would make their great-grandmother Georgia proud. I will draw on the spirit of my own great-grandmother Margaret, my grandmother Georgia, and Leila, and I will teach what has been taught to me because wherever you go, and whomever you love, home is always home and family is always family.

I will teach what has been taught to me because wherever you go, and whomever you love, home is always home and family is always family.

—Art

When we are young and ambitious we spread our wings. Eventually we land back at the nest, if only to gain a little perspective on how far we have traveled on our wonderful journeys. It can be a difficult trip, but it is one we all should make sometime in our lives if we have been away. Here's to returning back to family, and accepting our differences—as well as our similarities. Celebrate those special people along the way. I leave you with one great secret:

Choose to remember the good and celebrate it, and let go of the bad.

I hope that I meet you on my return back to my family. I wish you a safe journey back to yours.

XOXOXO

Art Smith

Acknowledgments

This journey all began with my own family—my beloved grandparents, aunts, uncles, and cousins of the Smith and Jones families. Our Sunday dinners and family gatherings inspired me to start my mission of teaching people the importance of sharing at the table, and getting back to the family.

Therefore, I would like to thank Grandmother Mable (ninety years old this year!) for the many years of love and great food; my mother, "Addie Mae," for teaching me to listen to the birds; my father for teaching me to surround myself with great people; my brother Gene, Anise, and all the children; Leslie and Don and the babies; Auntie Evelyn and Uncle Franklin; cousin Sharon Leonard; my Tallahassee family: Annella and Ron Schomburger; Ben, Lagrann, and Max; my darling Asbey Stiff; Dorothy Clifford; and Susan Turner.

Thanks to my great friends Adelay Suber, Nancy Petrandis, Nanette Fisher, Pierre and Rainey, chef Albert, my darling Annie B, Emily, Liz, Jerome, and all the other great people who shared their love with me. Thank you also to Josh Butler.

Thank you to my Chicago family and friends, who have made me feel so at home: Connie Pikalus, Linda Novick, P. J. Gray, Julie Bruyn and Naushab Ahmed, Margie Geddes, Tim and Phil, Manolis, Donna, Vinnie, Frana, Jamie and Patsy, and Charles and Andrea.

Thank you to Fredda Hyman and Diane Silverman, Thomas Pollak, Dan Watts and Vivian Valguarnera, Todd Hatoff, Fred Latsko and Julie, Carly Ubersox, and Bruce Seidel.

A big thank you to Rey Villalobos, my chef and the executive chef of TABLE restaurant; and also to Iris Davis and Ed Web, Sarah Levy, Jason Handelman, Jarred,

Jon Antony, Steve, Tammy, Miguel, Marvin and Roger, Potash Brothers Market, Daniel Lagarth and Kevin Fitzsimons.

Thank you to Stephen Hamilton and Raymond, Michael Austin, and my friends at Rutledge Hill Press: Geoffrey Stone and Pamela Clements. Thank you to Jan Miller and Nina, and all the wonderful people at Dupree, Miller.

Thank you to all the great people at the Oprah Winfrey Show: Jill B, Lisa E, Sherry Selata, Libby Moore, Novonna Cruz, Andre Walker, Angelic McFarland, Kelly Donnelly, Chris Hill, George Burns, Lisa Holiday, and Harriet Seitler; and to my friends at Oprah.com: Adam Glassman, Amy Gross, Gayle King, Jill D. Seelig, and Stefanie H. Maning.

Thank you as always to my beloved Oprah Winfrey and Stedman Graham.

Thank you to Dr. Jeffrey Raizer, our family doctor who kept our beloved Jesus Salgueiro close to us.

Thank you to Jesus Ramon Salgueiro, my friend and partner. I am grateful to you for your support of my work. Together we have done great things, and we will continue to do more, along with helping many people. Thank you also to your family: Andrea, David, and the children. I love you bundles.

Thank you everyone for your support and kindness through the years. I hope this book will be a tool, to bring many families back together. The world is full of goodness, and God gives us one family to share it with. Here's to celebrating the people who make up our families, and sharing a meal with them at the table.

From left to right: Rey Villalobos, sous chef; Jason Handleman, food stylist; Tom Hamilton, prop stylist; and Raymond Barrera, photo assistant.

Pantry, Kitchen Equipment, and Party Sources

The Lee Bros. Boiled Peanuts Catalogue

Charleston, S.C. • *843-720-8890*

A great source for southern food items with recommendations on fine, artisan products such as stone ground grits, corn meal, pickled green tomatoes, and Edwards Virginia hams. With the catalogue and *The Lee Bros. Southern Cookbook*, Matt and Ted Lee are the recognized authority on this regional cuisine.

Allen Brothers Catalogue

Chicago, Ill. • *800-548-2777*

America's most acclaimed butcher, Allen Brothers delivers to your door—anything from prime aged beef, American Wagyu, and veal to Colorado lamb, Berkshire pork, and apple wood-smoked bacon. They also offer many delicious heat-and-serve products. And in 2007, look for the Art Smith *Back to the Table* line of foods in the catalogue. Ask for my friend Todd Hatoff, the company president.

Fox & Obel Market

Chicago, Ill. • *312-410-7301*

This market houses the Midwest's largest selection of gourmet foods, olive oils, vinegar, artisan cheeses, truffle oil, Stonewall Kitchen Cranberry Mustard, Jamaican jerk seasoning, tapenade, dried cremini mushrooms, manchego cheese, Parmigiano-Reggiano, and Miguel & Valentino Apple Reduction. Ask for executive chef Jason Handelman.

Potash Brothers Market

Chicago, Ill. • *312-337-7537*

This is a great American family grocery store—the local grocer of choice for myself and my boss for more than twenty years. Here you can find late Riesling vinegar, Lucini Olive Oil, Laurent Du Clos Dijon Walnut Mustard, and amazing produce. Potash Brothers lettuce is the best for salads, always fresh from the field. Ask for Dave, Melvin, Sally or Art Potash. Also, Allan their wine buyer, is the best wine official of any grocery store in America.

Sarah's Pastries & Candies Inc.

Chicago, Ill. • *312-664-6223*

Sarah Levy is the Queen of Sweet. She by far makes the most delicious sweets of anyone in the Midwest. People line up to sample her chocolate clusters. Her cupcakes and cakes are the best. Ask for the beautiful Sarah Levy. She is always in the kitchen, so stop by her shop and tell her Art sent you.

Del Monte Foods

San Francisco, Calif.

America's most trusted purveyor of fine canned fruits and vegetables. Many recipes prepared in our cookbook use these high quality products. Also, look forward to their wonderful organic line of tomatoes and other products. Their fruit singles are the best. I love their Orchard Select, too. Del Monte products are available in supermarkets across the country.

Starkist Tuna

Pittsburgh, Penn.

I use the amazing vacuum-packed albacore white tuna for many of my dishes. The lemon pepper is my preferred choice of flavors. We all used canned tuna but this high-tech way to package it makes it taste much better.

Pete's Fresh Produce

Chicago, Ill. • 773-523-4600

Go to Pete's for Mexican food supplies. And don't forget to try their prepared foods, some of the best of any supermarket chain. What I love about these markets is that they are in the most diverse areas of Chicago's South Side, with absolutely amazing fresh produce, and great prices. Go there to find chile molido, ancho chile, guajillo chile, mild ground chile, chile de Arbol, poblano chile, queso fresco, Mexican chocolate, and many other great foods.

Global Palate

16 McGuirk Street • East Hampton, N.Y.

I found amazing spice blends in Loaves & Fishes, in Bridgehampton, N.Y. These blends are like no others I have ever had. Their tandoor spice is wonderful and they have many Asian blends that will make your dishes so incredibly tasty. All of their blends are freshly ground to order, which you can do online.

Sausages by Amy

Chicago, Ill. • 800-233-9629

These are the most delicious chicken sausages on the market. Created by the third-generation queen of one of Chicago's most acclaimed sausage-making families, these sausages have shown up in my dishes for years. I love to serve them for breakfast and put them in frittatas and jambalayas. Try all of their many flavors, available nationwide.

White Lily Flour

Knoxville, Tenn. • 800-264-5459

There are other southern flours, but don't even think about making a biscuit without this flour. My biscuits, cakes, and pies are the best mainly due to this great flour. It's been made for over a century, and many southern cooks have trusted it. I carry it with me wherever I am in the world. Try their corn bread mix and other products, too.

Fiji Water

Los Angeles, Calif. • 888-426-3454

Every party and dinner should start out with this fresh-tasting water—one of the best on the market. I sometimes wonder how a little island can produce so much great-tasting water. Just ask Jean-Georges, Charlie Trotter and many other great chefs—we all agree, it's the best. It is available nationwide, and they will deliver it to your home.

Beantrees Organic Coffee

Sacramento, Calif. • 916-451-3744

This free-trade coffee is the only one you will find in my home. I make a cappuccino every morning with it. I steam my organic milk and add two shots of espresso. Try it once and you will notice the difference in taste. A chef friend introduced me to it and I have never gone back. They have many beans from around the world, but my favorites are the beans from Timor.

Adagio Teas

These amazing teas were introduced to me by Evan Orensten of www.coolhunting.com. I adore the Jasmine Pearls, and the Yunnan Gold. There are many teas on the market but I have found these to be the freshest and some of the rarest. Also, try their bottled iced teas, with great tea flavor and without sugar, additives, or preservatives.

Palm Bay Imports

Boca Raton, Fla. • 561-362-9642

These folks are a large distributor of Cavit wines and other amazing Italian and Israeli wines. My friend Mike Wolf got me hooked on their fine wines, which you will find at every party I host in Chicago, and elsewhere in the United States for that matter.

Kitchen Equipment

Viking
Greenwood, Miss. • 888-VIKING1

There are many ranges and ovens out there, but very few are made in America by hard-working southern folks. After Hurricane Katrina devastated the Gulf Coast, I felt compelled to support the businesses of the region. Fred Carl has done great things in his community, plus he makes a wonderful range. His ovens bake my cakes beautifully. And we tested every recipe in this book using this equipment.

Bridge Kitchenwear
New York, NY • 800-274-3435

This is the source in Manhattan for everything for your home or restaurant kitchen. The Bridge family is the most trusted name in this business. Stephen, who took over the business from him parents, imports some of the best tools and knives anywhere. He is an encyclopedia of information about cooking. His manager Naushab Ahmed will also fill your ears with endless ways to use their tools. Every food personality in the know shops at this store. Just ask Martha Stewart or Mario Batali.

Sur La Table
Seattle, Wash. (and other locations nationwide)

This store is a great source for Staub, Le Creuset, All-Clad and many other great pots and pans for the home kitchen. Check their schedule to see what cooking star is stopping by to sign books or teach a cooking class. The store hosts America's most comprehensive in-store cooking class program, taught by in-house chefs, celebrity cookbook authors, and television cooking stars.

Poliform USA
New York, Chicago, Los Angeles • 877-VARENNA

The talented people in the Varenna kitchen division of Poliform USA are responsible for the creation of the incredible Italian-manufactured kitchen in my home in Chicago. Their kitchens are efficient and clean, not to mention beautiful.

Party Needs

Baumgartner & Co.
Chicago, Ill. • 312-770-9052

This is Chicago's premier florist, used by all of the city's movers and shakers. Lance, who does all of my flowers for important parties, is famous for his "villages of flowers"—beautiful specimen flowers in crystal vases, clustered on tables. Flowers are a very important part of daily living, and a party without them is down right sad.

A Perfect Event
Chicago, Ill. • 773-244-9333

Debi Lilly coordinates the parties I throw for clients as well as for friends and family, and she does not miss a detail—from monogrammed napkins custom-made for a single party to beautiful party favors for my guests. I first met her on the *Oprah Winfrey Show*, where for years she has been a guest. If you have a special wedding or birthday, Debi will make it unforgettable.

Tablescapes
Chicago, Ill. • 312-733-9700

This is the best party rental company in Chicago, and I have used them for everything from custom silver flatware to Riedel glassware, and every kind of base plate known to partydom. Cathy knows her business, and for years she has taken care of people who love to throw big parties but do not want to neglect the details that make the affair elegant.

Service Is Us, Inc.
Chicago, Ill. • 773-784-2225

Todd and Tripp have been providing the service on my *Oprah Winfrey Show* cooking segments for years. For me, a party is not a party unless I have them working it. The people they employ are not only beautiful, but also well versed in the tradition of fine service.

Index